CW01369532

FAITH

Michael Eigen

KARNAC

First published in 2014 by
Karnac Books Ltd
118 Finchley Road, London NW3 5HT

Copyright © 2014 to Michael Eigen

The right of Michael Eigen to be identified as the author of this work has been asserted in accordance with §§ 77 and 78 of the Copyright Design and Patents Act 1988.

All rights reserved. No part of this publication may be reproduced, stored in a retrieval system, or transmitted, in any form or by any means, electronic, mechanical, photocopying, recording, or otherwise, without the prior written permission of the publisher.

British Library Cataloguing in Publication Data

A C.I.P. for this book is available from the British Library

ISBN 978 1 78220 154 0

Edited, designed and produced by The Studio Publishing Services Ltd
www.publishingservicesuk.co.uk
e-mail: studio@publishingservicesuk.co.uk

Printed in Great Britain

www.karnacbooks.com

CONTENTS

ACKNOWLEDGEMENTS vii

ABOUT THE AUTHOR ix

PREFACE AND INTRODUCTION xi

CHAPTER ONE
Can goodness survive life? 1

CHAPTER TWO
Moments that count 9

CHAPTER THREE
On Winnicott 23

CHAPTER FOUR
Winnicott: an added note 37

CHAPTER FIVE
What is evil? 41

CHAPTER SIX
Tiger stripes and student voices 55

CHAPTER SEVEN
Variants of mystical participation 77

CHAPTER EIGHT
No one can save you from the work that you have 91
to do on yourself

CHAPTER NINE
Jumping in 107

CHAPTER TEN
Future as unknown presence (even if it is absent) 121

AFTERWORD
Faith-work 123

REFERENCES 125

INDEX 129

ACKNOWLEDGEMENTS

I should like to express my thanks for permission to reprint in this book the following material.

Chapter Two, "Moments that count" first appeared in *Clinical Implications of the Psychoanalyst's Life Experience: When the Personal Becomes Professional*, S. Kuchuck (Ed.). New York: Routledge, 2014.

Chapter Three, "On Winnicott" first appeared as "On Winnicott's clinical innovations in the analysis of adults." *International Journal of Psychoanalysis* (2012) 93: 1449–1459.

Chapter Four, "Winnicott: an added note" was first published as "Response by Michael Eigen" in *International Journal of Psychoanalysis* (2013) 94: 118–121.

Chapter Six, "Tiger stripes and student voices". A short version of this may appear in *Teaching Bion*, M. H. Williams (Ed.). London: Karnac.

Chapter Seven, "Variants of mystical participation" first appeared in *Shared Realities: Participation Mystique and Beyond*, M. Winborn (Ed.). Fisher King Press, 2014.

Chapter Eight, "No one can save you from the work that you have to do on yourself." Interview by Micha Odenheimer. *Eretz Acheret* ("Another Country"), 2005, 5(26): 36–42.

Chapter Nine, "Jumping in", is based on an interview by J. C. Niemera, "Interview with Michael Eigen", *Psychoanalytic Perspectives* (2011) *8*: 259–270. Used with permission of the National Institute for the Psychotherapies.

Chapter Ten, "Future as unknown presence (even if it is absent)". *The Candidate* (2012) 5(1).

ABOUT THE AUTHOR

Michael Eigen worked with disturbed, especially psychotic, children in his twenties, then adults in his thirties and onwards. He directed an institute programme for working with creative individuals at the Center for Psychoanalytic Training and was the first Director of Educational Training at the Institute for Expressive Analysis. He was on the Board of Directors at the National Psychological Association for Psychoanalysis for eight years, first as Program Chair, then editor of *The Psychoanalytic Review*. He has taught at many institutes and colleges and given talks and seminars internationally. In the past twenty years, he taught and supervised mainly at the National Psychological Association for Psychoanalysis and the New York University Postdoctoral Program in Psychotherapy and Psychoanalysis. He gives a private seminar on Winnicott, Bion, Lacan, and his own work, ongoing for nearly forty years. *Faith* is his twenty-fourth book.

Preface and Introduction

What is faith? Not a question I can answer but I am poor at answering many questions. How can I write about something without knowing what it is? Without being able to say what it is? Yet it is, at least, so I feel. But faith is more than feeling, at times not even feeling. A felt sense, but not just a felt sense. A mode of cognition? A mode of experiencing? Part of the atmospheric condition of psychic being that helps support the work of other capacities? Premonition? Intimation?

In *Faith and Transformation* (2011a) I distinguish faith from belief. Too often, I find belief killing faith. People fight over beliefs, my belief *vs.* your belief. Faith as structured by belief systems that bring people together, create chasms, turn people against each other. I would like to distinguish faith from the way other capacities try to organise it.

We might say faith spans many dimensions. Natural faith, religious faith, faith in life, in oneself, in others. Faith *vs.* cynicism. Possibly even cynical faith. Sometimes, I picture faith as a kind of generic emptiness which can assume many guises, many colours, fuse with all kinds of identities and ideologies. Is nationalism a kind of faith or anti-faith, a defence against faith? A way of organising life so as to miss the essential life of faith, to miss one's encounter with faith?

Rainbow of faith, hope, care. The fact of colour that brings wonder and joy. Colour thrills us. Have you ever felt colour running through your body, permeating you? Like sound? Music?

What is it colour and music try to express if not a sacral sense that binds us to being and takes us beyond it, through it? Keats: spirit ditties of no tone. Yeats: soul clap its hands and sings. One hand clapping, thunderous, electric no-sound, just so. Where is faith? Do you see it in fish swimming in a stream? Or perhaps just the stream itself? Is it in the cracks, the pores? Where is it not, often is asked. But, in real life, we find many places that seem to sink it, poison it, maim and, yes, kill it. Can faith die? Are there conditions in which it cannot be born? Does the human spirit die or fail to be born?

Naïve faith, sophisticated faith, critical faith. Faith with infinite dimensions and no location at all. Where is it hiding? I want to say we are living in it but I cannot speak for everyone.

"Love God with all your heart, with all your soul, with all your might." To live in this place. "The Place"—*Hamakom*—a Hebrew name for God, associated with freedom. Love God with all you are—does that come close to saying what faith is? Faith unites, binds, frees? There is a faith that aches to get closer and closer, a faith that aches to be born.

Life lives in faith, faith permeates life, every single cell. That does not exclude faithlessness, no-faith, the empty bottom.

And psychoanalytic faith? The work of faith in sessions? As I brought out in *Toxic Nourishment* (1999), many sessions are crises of faith. Is life worth living? With what quality? How? Or is a soul too crippled to go on, too infected with ill spirit?

Does psychoanalytic faith involve faith in therapy? Does one need faith in therapy to be in therapy and profit from it? Or is faith something to be earned by the hard work that therapy can involve? One develops more faith by experiencing openings of self, by experiencing possibility.

One psychoanalyst, Wilfred R. Bion, calls the psychoanalytic attitude Faith—he writes it with a capital F. He amplifies Freud's free-floating attention by attempting to characterise the psychoanalytic attitude as a practice of being without memory, expectation, understanding, or desire. One might say such a state of affairs is not possible. But as an attitude, a path, it can open possibilities of growth one might not have found otherwise.

Bion, too, allies faith with growth of intuition. He sometimes characterises psychic life as ineffable, immaterial, unlocalisable. He sometimes writes of psychoanalytic intuition as beyond sensory experience, an open capacity that can register emotional impacts and help initiate digestion of experience. He allies intuition with attention. The more attention paid to a field of experience, the more one sees, the more it seems to grow. The more glimpses of psychic reality, the more psychic reality there is to glimpse. Faith as an opening to psychic reality. Faith as inherent support for attention.

* * *

The chapters of this book explore nuances of faith–no-faith moments, twists and turns of living. Chapter One, "Can goodness survive life?", is based on a talk I gave for the First World Humanities Forum, 2011. Experience of natural beauty and awe, deep peace of dreamless sleep, void states, and erotic fullness are moments that arouse implicit faith in the goodness of life, a faith that takes many traumatic hits. Can a sense of goodness survive life's destructiveness? We may chase our tails with such a question, but realities of pain and beauty sear our beings.

Chapter Two, "Moments that count", first appeared in *Clinical Implications of the Psychoanalyst's Life Experience: When the Personal Becomes Professional,* edited by Steven Kuchuck. It moves from important faith experiences in my early twenties with writings of Thomas Merton and Paul Tillich through encounters with Winnicott and Bion in my thirties and forties. Reading and meeting these great psychoanalysts added to the multi-dimensional work of faith in my life. Bion played an important role in my getting married and becoming a father as well, a momentous transformational happening.

Chapters Three and Four are writings exploring D. W. Winnicott's contributions for the *International Journal of Psychoanalysis.* Reading and meeting Winnicott changed my life, added to it. I try to bring out aspects of this extended encounter that were, and continue to be, enriching. An implicit faith element is an important part of Winnicott's life and work. He speaks of a vital spark that needs and seeks nourishment, a spark that is part of everyday faith and creativity, a spark with a special kind of thrill and challenge. Like Bion, he is very much engaged in working with survival and growth of creative living in interaction with destructive currents. As an aside, I included Clare

Winnicott's letter to me, sent when my "Area of faith" (1981a) paper came out. In it, she spoke of how the "use of object" reality her husband portrayed played out in their lives together, adding freshness, a creative spark.

Chapter Five, "What is evil?", solves no problems but turns the question and reality of evil around in many directions, inside out and outside in, interacting with experience of pain, destruction, horror, resilience, and creative possibilities. We are scarred by evil within and without and by our formulations of evil as well. I depict a man I worked with who saw devils and heard pronouncements from a devil-god who bossed him around, making him feel bad for not being able to follow the most destructive commandments, which would result in murder and suicide. What seemed like eternal, immovable commandments turned out to be made of processes we could interact with by imaginative attention and our growing relationship. A crucial issue that is part of this matrix has to do with condemning oneself for weakness which, on many occasions, has a positive function, for example, being too weak to kill oneself, a stranger, a neighbour, a loved one. One is persecuted inwardly for lack of courage, for being weak, a condition that, paradoxically, may be on the side of life.

At times, it takes faith to express oneself. At times, it takes even more faith to wait and let further processes develop. The biblical Cain is criticised for failing to do the latter, acting precipitously, partly as a defence against letting something deeper happen. Sometimes, action short-circuits more complex psychic invagination, and sometimes it adds to experiential possibilities. Our many rich capacities take on value depending on use in variable situations.

This chapter also includes variations of a basic pattern that exercises Bion, how good moments turn bad. As part of our discussion, I use his description of feeling a sissy in the face of pain, a feeling that scarred his life no matter how courageous he was or made of steel he became. The weak, sensitive boy plagued him as well as fed his creativity. His writing, like Rumi's, welcomes the many "guests" that occupy his house and, a bit like Pinter or Beckett, at times dramatically portrays them.

Chapter Six, "Tiger stripes and student voices," elaborates on experiences of teaching Bion, for student and teacher. A shorter version of this chapter may be in *Teaching Bion*, edited by Meg Harris Williams, who has written telling works on Bion (2010, 2013).

I began teaching Bion to learn from him, a learning process that continues to this moment. His work with psychosis, explorations of deep links between catastrophe and faith, work with dream and myth, the inarticulate, and more touched my core. My private seminar, ongoing for forty years, gives me chance to dig in and get as far as I can go, an atmosphere in which we speak creatively. This chapter explores many variations of faith. Aspects of reality keep rotating, truths of experiencing keep emerging. In this case, not only my words, but those of students. I asked students if any were interested in writing on their experience of our seminar. As many quotes as could reasonably fit the chapter's space were included.

Chapter Seven, "Variants of mystical participation," was originally published in *Shared Realities: Participation Mystique and Beyond*, edited by Mark Winborn. It depicts moments that span a spectrum from mystical through shifting nuances of heightened states, alone and with another. Two series of moments, far apart yet with commonalities, involve experiences of eye-lock with a girlfriend and a hyena. Have you had moments where your eyes lock with the eyes of another, moments that go on and on without a seeming end in sight? When this happened with a young woman I was seeing, it felt as if heart and soul lock as well as eyes, the latter truly gateway to the soul. Yet, something similar happened with a hyena, not with soul and heart, but an interlocking neither of us could or wanted to tear away from. A heightened state that glued us together in fear and wonder.

We journey through heightened moments opened by capacities imaged by the Kabbalah Tree of Life, not so much diagrams of our souls as souls in action, including soul and heart in everyday life, in one case, a grandfather with his grandson. Weaving through gradations of linking moments, the chapter climaxes with Rabbi Yohai's (hero of the *Zohar*) marriage with the *Shechinah* (the Bride, the Holy Presence) at the moment of his death.

Chapter Eight, "No one can save you from the work that you have to do on yourself", is based on an interview Micha Odenheimer did with me for *Eretz Acheret* ("Another Land"), 2005. Micha burrows in on my interest in Catholicism and meetings with a number of "gurus" at different phases of my life, with particular emphasis on spiritual experience, including meetings with Rabbi Kellner, Rabbi Menachem Schneerson, Allen Ginsberg, Muktananda, Chongyam Trungpa, D. W. Winnicott, and Wilfred Bion. He seemed to want me to talk about transcendent mystical experience, but I kept tying spirituality to the here and now, how one is with other people and how one treats oneself. This must have led the publisher to subtitle the interview: "About the spirituality branded in the intimate encounters of human suffering".

Micha then asked about the state of America today, which opened the door to discussing a kind of psychopathic spirit or attitude, in some ways a world spirit, but certainly an important streak in human nature, a theme further elaborated in Chapter Nine. We ended the interview returning to the importance of what one gains from others and how it can free one to be oneself, a paradoxical situation. Through others one finds one's own voice, one's own way of being a problematic being, with the particular touch and taste one brings to life.

Chapter Nine, "Jumping in", is based on an interview Jan Niemera did for *Psychoanalytic Perspectives*, 2011, in conjunction with his book review of *Flames from the Unconscious: Trauma, Madness, and Faith*. He zeros in on my early experience of being a therapist and seminars I gave, an outburst of British psychoanalysis in New York, at first Winnicott and later Bion. Becoming a therapist seemed more timeless, unrushed then, more steeping time and less invasion by administrative and economic pressures. One could be more engaged with the work itself and be supported in doing so. Now, I think, many have to spend more time on extrinsic demands, and push against the tide not to sacrifice intrinsic quality.

Jan's questioning moves further into issues raised by the work itself. One of the cases in *Flames from the Unconscious* is a woman who suffered multiple hospitalisations but, through long-term therapy, became hospital and medication free. Her journey brings out complexities of many double tendencies, tensions between fear of being alone, fear of being with others, and our need for both; fear of being a child, fear of being an adult, and need for both; confusion and sometimes paralysis in face of the multiplicity we are, including our proliferating or stultifying identificatory capacity, an amazing capacity that dumbfounds and exhilarates; learning to work with fullness and void states and how they are organised in different people. The demands and gift of multi-dimensional complexity can be dizzying, but this is part of the garden we are given to tend, to partner.

We speak of an age-old doubleness that is more crucial than ever, the need to be self-and-other orientated. As discussed in Chapter

Eight, emphasis on self has spiralled, as witnessed by economic psychopathy at the expense of care for others. At the same time, an affiliative tendency plays a role in personal and social life in many ways. In therapy, we have a chance to explore multi-directional tendencies that often are acted on blindly, a venture very much in progress.

And if we find something that works, its very working may change the situation in ways that require a fresh start. We often come to a place that cannot be worked with, yet trying to find one's way with unsure instruments is part of what makes this work gruelling and thrilling, and often part of what helps us grow.

Chapter Ten, "Future as unknown presence (even if it is absent): fragmentary notes on time experience in therapy", published by *The Candidate*, a student journal. Time, like silly putty, can be turned or twisted every which way. All time is now, no time now. One speaks a lot about the past or present in clinical work, but future, also, is a strong presence (absence). Where does the future go in sessions, not just long term but waiting on the next moment, a moment that might never come or become the painful or blissful unexpected. Future as stimulus of birth of creativeness or the improvisatory next moment that brings us to unimagined places as well as places we know and fear too well. Sessions that creep or race by might have different sensations of the future. Sometimes, the future questions us: who will you become, how, when? Often, when people speak of having faith in life, they mean faith in the future, what kind of future, with what quality? The future can ambush you, take you by the hand, lead, crush, swallow, embrace, fly by.

The ten chapters are followed by an Afterword consisting of a short statement called "Faith-work", reworking passages from Chapter Six, on teaching–learning Bion. Faith, for Bion the psychoanalytic attitude, meets catastrophic realities and opens paths of growth.

* * *

All of the chapters in this book, with one exception, were written in the past three years. By the time this book is published I will be eighty, or nearly so. I have written a lot about my twenties, thirties, and forties, moments of meaning. However, the past several years have involved deepening and opening of experience I scarcely thought possible. By the time this book reaches you, more than I can say here will have happened and, I hope, be happening. It cannot be otherwise. One cannot grab life by the tail and tell it to stop, and why would one want to? The writing here remains a testament to life lived, ways I have grappled with life and ways I have been moved, an alive process that goes on living, form to form. I hope you will take these words as a sharing of something precious, something needed, something true. And beneath them a faith that struggles through forms to touch the unseen that touches us.

Psychoanalysis challenges us to build capacity to support emotional life without resorting to violence—although experiencing emotional life itself can be violent. Some go through more than they can bear in order to grow. I suspect the possibility of growth in the face of, and while undergoing, destructive impacts is part of what led Bion to posit Faith as the psychoanalytic attitude. There are ways, I fear, that faith can grow by being ripped apart. Faith that strengthens by being nulled, that takes us to unanticipated places when there is no cause for it to exist at all. (Eigen, *A Felt Sense*)

Faith in face of catastrophic inner–outer reality. An extraordinary nucleus in the depths of feeling life. An emotional nucleus that is part of a basic rhythm: breaking, shattering, going under, dying, and coming through. This is what faith faces, must face. It is germane to the fervour and possibility of existence, a tension, struggle, sense that has an impact on the flavour of our lives. (Eigen, *Faith*)

Faith plays an important role in transformational processes. I don't mean "belief". Belief may be a necessary part of the human condition but it tends to prematurely organise processes that remain unknown. Faith supports exploration, imaginative conjecture, experiential probes. The more we explore therapy, the more we appreciate how much our response capacity can grow. We are responsive beings, for good and ill. Too often, our responses hem us in. We short-circuit growth of responsiveness. Yet, it is possible to become aware of the rich world our responsive nature opens, places it takes us, feelings with as yet no name, hints of contact that may never be exhausted. (Eigen, *Faith and Transformation*)

There is love we have no words for, something touched perhaps by phrases like "love of God", a love that precipitates a crises of faith, a crises of faith that lifts existence. ("Paraphrasing" Bion, *Faith*)

Michael Eigen: In Ireland I saw a bell in a case that said it had the purest sound in the world. It was in a case and no one heard it ring.

I listened with all my might and heard a silent ring within we share.

Rachel Berghash: No one heard the ring of the bell, yet considered the purest sound in the world, sounds like faith. (Posts in a Yahoo workshop)

Out of the depths I call (cry) to You . . . (Psalm 130)

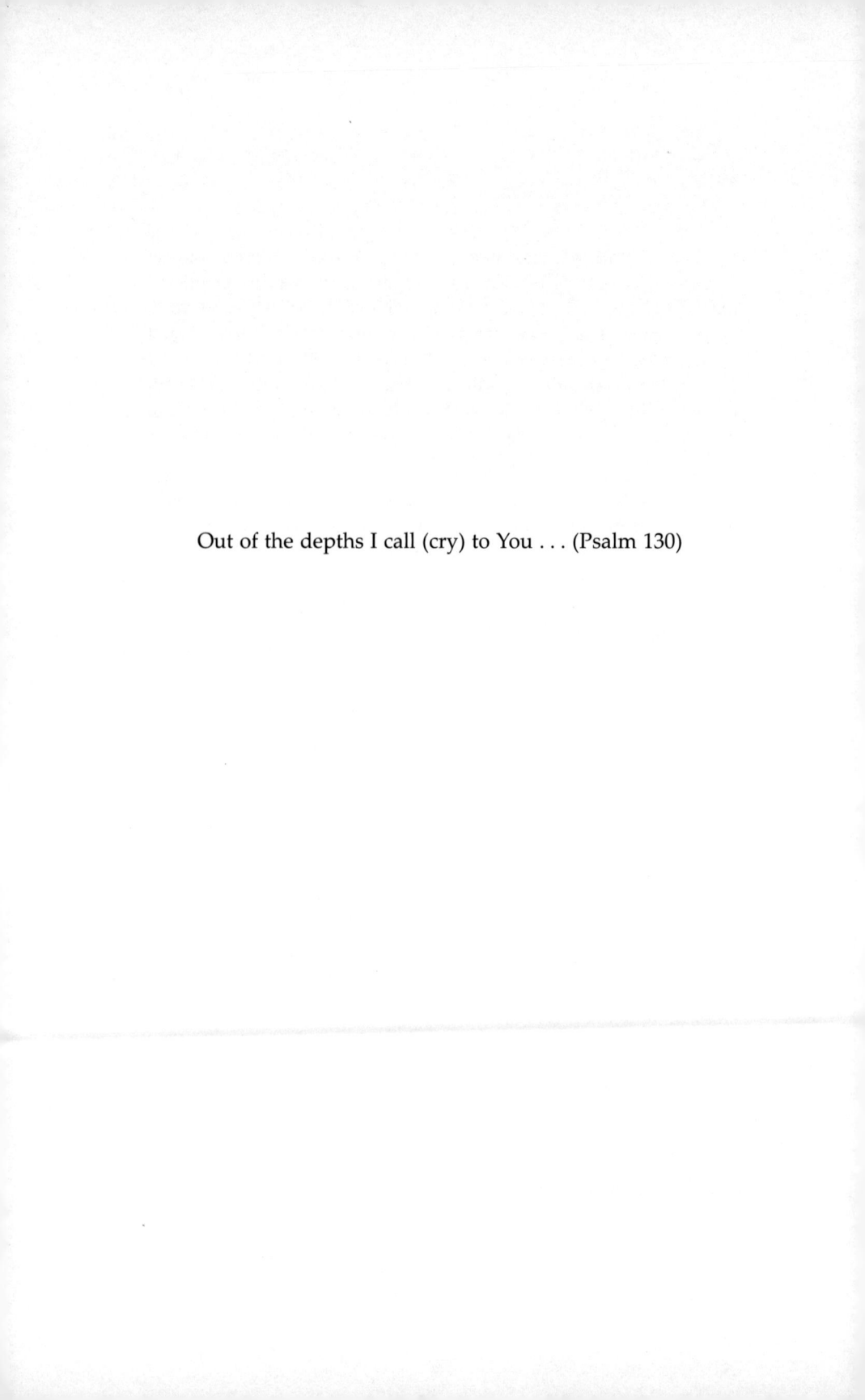

CHAPTER ONE

Can goodness survive life?

Beauty, I believe, is one source of ethics. To see something beautiful can arouse a sense of goodness. Not only a sense of feeling good, but also a sense of wanting to do right by, wanting to do justice to, a world which can be so beautiful, which can so touch one to the depths. Tears of beauty. As Keats says, "A thing of beauty is a joy forever". An ethics with roots in beauty and joy. Tears of joy, happiness, at times, awe. The world in its uplifting aspect, world as inspiration. An ethics of beauty, joy, inspiration, creativity.

I am thinking now of moments of beauty fused with awe on viewing the great rocks at Yosemite Park in California (Eigen, 2006a). Yosemite silenced me. Words dissolved. A wordless world for millions of years. Mammoth rocks, mammoth stars. God's beauty. Tears of awe. The soul of the rock says, "Come closer."

I find a link between such stillness and awe while awake and the deep peace of dreamless sleep. For a psychoanalyst, dreaming is important. Dreaming plays a role in psychic digestion, emotional digestion. Yet, dreaming speaks to us through fragmented narrative structures. Awe in the face of Yosemite seems more immediate. Dreams feed us affective narratives we can work with while awake. They are rarely still. They have a certain speed, like fish swimming in water. They may rush by before you catch them or even glimpse them. Sometimes you "know" them only by their ripples. The deep stillness and awe evoked in Yosemite takes me to another place.

We sleep not only to dream, but to allow contact with places dreaming cannot reach, that reach towards dreaming. Bion (1992) suggests one reason sleep is essential is to make possible emotional experiences the personality cannot have while awake. Sleep enables experience outside the reach of waking and dreaming to move towards dreaming's reach. This coheres with the Hindu saying that everyday life is the past, dreaming is the present, and dreamless void the future.

Shall we call this a wordless, imageless unconscious, a portal through which our lives are fed impalpably and ineffably by experience that accesses us in dreamless sleep? As though God or nature or evolution has safeguarded something from our use of it, a special form of contact that we cannot ruin with our controlling narratives, or our lust for power, or our fears, which gains access to us when our ordinary focus and selective attention, even the foci of our dreams, are out of play. A contact that accesses us when we are not looking (Eigen, 2011a). How can something touch us if we are not aware of it? An aporia that marks our existence, our plasticity, perhaps marks us with a sense of mystery.

The peace found in dreamless sleep gives us something most dreams cannot provide. It takes us deeper than conflict, antagonism, fear. So many dreams have persecutory elements, distilling and exaggerating frictions of waking life. Where does the idea of peace come from? One source, I feel, is the profundity of sleep. The association of "profound" with sleep is no accident. That sleep can be profound gifts us with a deep sense of peace that daily anxieties cannot exhaust. A peace we might fail to access while awake but which enters while we are asleep. We look forward to sleep after a day of activity, not just to refresh ourselves, but to contact the deep peace that rest and sleeping can bring. A peace we may try to tap and even base ourselves on through prayer and meditation.

There are threads in waking life that reverberate with the ineffable background of our beings. The thunderous silence of Yosemite, a wordless awe, feels connected to the impalpable portal in dreamless sleep that freshens life. An awesome peace stirring in Yosemite grandeur. A stirring peace embedded in heights of awakening and depths of sleep. There are different kinds of peace. I am interested in an enlivening one. Peace that stirs, lifts. It is not just that I am little and Yosemite is big, or that we are both changing and passing, slowly or quickly. We are both amazing in spirit, the great spirit of the rock, my thrilling awareness of the rock, a stirred and stirring awareness. Coming alive, shivering by being touched by, invaded by, stone. A grandeur that transfers to ordinary experience that is part of the touch of flesh.

There are great ideas that link up with this profound stirring. For me, Plato's vision of the Good is one, Kant's treating each other as ends, not just means, is another. These ideas link with the golden rule, giving, caring, putting oneself in the place of the other. Kant speaks of the moral universe as more thrilling than the starry skies. Where does the idea of peace, caring, treating others as ends come from in a world permeated by survival needs, practicality, antagonisms, lust for power?

Levinas (1969; Eigen, 2005) touches another possibility, expressed in response to the human face. An ethical sense inscribed in our flesh, growing through our experience of the other, particularly another's expressive face.

Levinas writes of a vulnerability, an infinite appeal, even a destitution. The other calls for our response. We are not speaking of the other as master now, or slave, but the other as naked before God, as naked to others, needy, yes, but also at risk. We ask something of others and it is that something we are required to give. An infinite asking, an infinite giving. Neither term can be exhausted.

What Levinas speaks of is the appeal of faces everywhere, universal appeal, a concrete universal embedded in experience. An immediate appeal that experience is made of. No exclusions. This is the ethical aim inscribed in our looking, hearing, feeling bodies, the aim that lifts us, impels us into life beyond murder. An impossibility, perhaps. But when we sense it we know that Kant is right, it is a beauty the stars themselves sing to. A happening that brings a smile to every infant's heart and face, a spontaneous smile in response to another, alive with expressive, touching radiance—unless something has gone horribly wrong.

What, then, are we called on to give? We are asked to give ourselves. To give of ourselves. And for this, no one else will do. There are no substitutes for what only you bring now, this particular, passing forever.

An enfleshed infinite, an immediate infinite, infinite immediacy: from an infant's response to its mother's face, to our response as grown-ups to each other. An infinite immediacy that embraces, that upholds within it as its nucleus an infinite distance, intimate distance that calls for respect as well as caring. To see and sense as a form of giving. How can distance be an infinite immediacy, an inexhaustible caring? Doesn't distance run the range from cruel to compassionate? To live a difference that does justice to what is lived: isn't this an immediacy worth striving for?

We have had time to learn how injury is inflicted, to read the pain we create in one before us. To behead the enemy, the stranger, to destroy the intimate: we know these well. We are an abusive species, a tormented species, a pain-inflicting group. We know how defensive we are, warding off the pain that is our heritage, that comes at us from all directions. We know, too, what it is like to support life in one in need. To come through ourselves, to help. Have we decided as a group which is the greater satisfaction, the greater prompting? Have we decided to water down the appeal—a mutual appeal—that brings life to another level?

Which do we imagine the greater fear: that we will be empty if not brutal, or empty if not giving? We dread losing either way, as if we need both to feel alive, a dependency, an addiction to the dialectics of brutality and giving. Part of suicide bombing's compelling genius is that both poles maximally combine: the flash of brutality and fullness of self-giving. Giving oneself to God or cause, supported in the background by devoted faces, friends, mother, militant brothers. The flaw: to believe some faces are human, some are not.

Financial "suicide bombers" are harder to pin down because devotion to a cause larger than themselves is often lacking. Or is the larger "cause" big business, money, and power, so-called "self-interest", an economic monster run amok. Compulsive success in making and controlling wealth spirals to a point destructive of the welfare of many, even destructive of the psychological–spiritual well being of "winners". Ethical and practical safeguards that might help regulate abuse are disregarded and abandoned. The explosion does not take the form of visible bombs (unless they are part of a war machine that both saps and nourishes the economy), but financial brinkmanship and breakdown resulting in catastrophic erosion of human spirit, life, and resources.

We began with awe, deep peace, stillness in waking life and sleep, our caring response to aspects of nature and the human face but, inevitably, find ourselves talking about destructiveness. Talk about goodness and destruction appears. As if we are, in part, constituted of a double helix in which our response to beauty and need to destroy intertwine.

Is it surprising that destruction plays so important a role in our lives, given that we live in a universe made up, partly, of explosive processes? We can try to personalise it, coat it with motivation, cause, agency. Wounds, power highs, territoriality, survival, triumph, victory, and defeat. The "who" varies. I beat you, you beat me. Subject–object pronouns vary, but the link, the "beat", remains the same. X allied with Y against Z allied with N.

X, Y, Z, N vary but *allied against* is invariant. Structures of destruction remain constant, although conditions change.

I sometimes wonder if our products make us claustrophobic. We feel hemmed in by what we make, worlds we build, and destruction feels like freedom. We need to destroy what we create in order to escape feeling trapped by our creations.

There is, too, a feeling that beauty hides ugly realities. Something may look good on the outside. Look a little closer, like eyes getting used to the dark, and you begin to see graves, bodies, blood, rabid injustices that support a good-looking city, or face, or work. Some feel it just to destroy the show of beauty, the make-believe, and get to how things really work, realities of power.

What can psychoanalysis contribute in an Age of Economic Psychopathy? Not much, I fear, but it does offer explorations in the cracks. It begins to confront, sustain, and work with destruction between human beings in ways not quite touched before. A question in deep analytic encounter is whether two human beings can survive each other and more, whether a human being can survive him- or herself—and how well.

In therapy, moment-to-moment exchange or sensing of feeling has time and room to breathe. A thread in these feelings involves mutual destruction. I destroy you; you destroy me. We are killers, one or another way. In therapy, we trace murderous impulses, see how they move, work, the forms they take, how they function, what they contribute to the psyche as a whole. Self-destruction and mutual destruction cannot be written off as by-products of attachment difficulties, although the latter can intensify them. They seem ingrained in human nature, a part of who we are. What we do with the destructive side of our nature is an open question. As of now, for the most part, we do not know what to do with it, and making believe we have answers postpones fuller struggle with the question. Jesus comes closest when he says, "Forgive them, father. They don't know what they're doing." We do not know what we are doing and pretending we do compounds the problem.

To kill the other and the other survives; to be killed and survive. This is one of the psychic paradoxes that therapy opens: to be killed and survive well; to kill and the other survives well. Therapy is training in dying and coming back to life, mutual dying and coming to life. This double movement is part of what I call a rhythm of faith. Faith makes this movement endurable, possible, at the same time faith is an outgrowth of mutual coming through.

By faith, I do not mean belief. We literally kill each other over beliefs. Faith supports experiencing and exploration of experience. Faith is deeper than belief. Belief often functions as premature organisation, closure of faith. One way that faith goes beyond belief is by enabling unknown transformations that open reality, transformations we may sense but are unable to pin down. Meditation, for example, can take us to places that have no names. We try not to interfere with nameless, imageless movements that change us as they happen.

Therapeutic faith supports engagement with destructive urges. In time, we begin to catch on, get an "inkling", a "feel" for processes involved in surviving murder, double murder. Can the therapy couple survive each other? And with what quality? Therapy is growth in quality of coming through. With what quality do *you* survive *yourself*?

In therapy, we build capacity to endure being with each other through mutual murder, death, renewal—a basic rhythm that is often aborted, often to the detriment of people's lives. In therapy, murder, death, and renewal is lived in terms of emotional reality. Actual, literal murder would abort the process. Literal murder short-circuits the build-up of capacity to tolerate the waxing and waning of feeling. Literal murder substitutes for the hard work of building capacity to tolerate emotional life and begin dreaming and working with the latter.

We can try to solve all the social problems we can. Relieve poverty and hunger, racial and sexual inequities—all to the good. But do not be surprised if the loose card in the deck, emotional life, finds ways to sabotage at least part of what is built. I write, in *Feeling Matters*, that as long as feelings are second-class citizens, people will be second-class citizens. Without work in the trenches of our nature, we may wreck what we try to create.

Struggling with oneself is one ingredient, but I am not speaking of the traditional "control" model. Controlling one's "animal", or "lower", or "recalcitrant" nature has had some value in controlling the masses and regulating destruction to an extent. But the lasting recurrence of wars, prisons, and exacerbated inequities involving "upper–lower" seem to add to problems they try to solve. Struggle is necessary, but I am speaking of more than struggle, something more akin to developing psychic taste buds. Developing a capacity to taste and work with experience, to give all voices of experience a say. Developing capacity to let experiencing build: a model less of control than of partnership, becoming partners with our capacities and evolving together.

A perennial challenge, more so today than ever, is the time and work that go into encoding goodness into daily living. Can goodness survive life, our lives? Inform our lives? Good people have tried for a long time to make goodness count. To an extent, they succeed, even as life sweeps much of their efforts away. To a certain extent, we are stymied, since the will to do good often harms.

The Bible is not just about lust for life or will to survive. It is about the struggle of goodness to survive, to make life better, the ever-besieged need to treat each other in better ways. The Bible sets goals such as "do not kill each other", but fails to show us how. Even God becomes exasperated and tries to wipe us out. I pointed out, in a book titled *Rage* (2002), that God's personality provides a case example, a telling picture of our destructive realities. God's tendency to wipe us out is our own tendency to wipe ourselves out, as if we can wipe out the problem of destruction with destruction.

No one has the answers. We cannot tell ahead of time what the outcome of decisions or actions will be. We need many kinds of contributions, science, art, politics, all walks of life. I do feel psychoanalysis adds something to the brew. In psychoanalysis, we learn a little more about destruction. We learn, or think we learn, that feelings matter, that we are sensitive beings who need to sense how sensitivity works, that ethics has roots in sensitivity to ourselves and others.

Psychoanalysis does not have the answers either, but provides avenues for exploring new forms of dialogue, new probes, new ventures of spirit. It, at least, highlights the difficulties and challenges our enigmatic, packed psyche brings.

Antagonism is everywhere: at boundaries between groups and individuals, in families, nations, within the self. A certain antagonism is part of our psychic immune system. As Kant has it, we are a sort of unsocial social group. Our protective hostility easily runs amok, like fantasy porcupines inflicting injury while trying to keep warm.

Yet, there is a seed of unquenchable optimism in our sea of pessimistic realism. Are we not catching on that it is up to us to work with the equipment we have been given, to partner our capacities, not just exploit them, to learn and keep on learning about our make-up? Is that not what we have been trying to do for thousands of years, probably longer? Is that not where evolution is taking us—closer to opposing our need to murder (whether physical, economic, social, or spiritual)? Closer to embracing the struggle with our make-up and trying to do better?

Psychoanalysis is one attempt to see what we can do if we open more boxes, combining models of control with models of affective exploration and emotional transmission. Whatever limitations and failures, psychoanalysis addresses aspects of psychic reality that must be grappled with. Attempts to outlaw or ban the psyche—by science, spirit, laughter, shouting, activism, or inaction—delay the work that has to be done. Work unknown. We cannot bully the psyche out of existence.

We glimpse ways of being together that I do not think quite existed before. Ways of feeling each other, exercising emotional taste buds, modes of relating that encompass but are more interesting than beating each other down. A cutting edge of evolution involves what it is like for people to be together. Affective attitude is a raw material shaping us as we shape it, creating richly textured possibilities of being. To listen, sense, and speak: a long journey ahead, no less important than reshaping colours, material forms, genes, and neural chemicals. Evolution of hearing, sensing, speaking: evolution materiality now depends on. Our sense of value and worth depend on this evolution.

CHAPTER TWO

Moments that count

In my twenties, the following two statements helped to orientate me. The first, by Thomas Merton: "The secret of our identity is in God's mercy". The second, by Paul Tillich: "A man is only as big as the diabolic in himself he can assimilate".

Such deep relief I felt on reading the first. Such challenge, on reading the second. The two together provided support and direction.

The secret of our identity is divine mercy. It is hard to describe the relief and uplift this brought. To think that mercy, loving kindness of the Other, is the heart of my being, not my own strident efforts and struggles. At the heart of my struggle was divine love. I did not have to do everything or "know" who I was. Each time I tried to know myself, identity faded from view. Ego chasing its tail, like the tail of a disappearing dog. But God's mercy? A sense that God's love was deeper than self gave me support, buoyed me. The pain of being an individual, of having to know who I was, dissolved in the enigma of being supported by infinite love. I felt myself more fully through this love than by frenetic efforts to be someone. A deep pain of my being met bottomless care: solution-less pain momentarily lessened, at times dissolved, when it touched divine mystery, love deeper than pain.

The second statement also relieved, but its challenge grew. To assimilate the diabolic in myself: a tall order. What if I was a devil or partly so? Assimilate myself? I knew the mythic theme of turning bad into good, the alchemical formula, base into rare. A radical theme of the story of Jesus: turn life into death, death into life. Or Freud's version of the great spiritual dare: id into ego.

Renunciation seemed part of spirituality. To transcend or transform lower into higher was part of spiritual paths, east and west. To transcend oneself, transform oneself. What can this mean? If I was diabolic, what do I give up, renounce, remove, transform? My I? Surely that is not all that is afflicted. All the psychic twists, deformations, wounds, horrors, and pleasures of self-centred lies?

Yet, Tillich's words freed me. Even if the task was impossible, it was a relief to hear his words. They validated the demonic and gave a kind of permission to acknowledge one's makeup. The demonic is real, part of human being. People are devils; devils are people. I am not alone in needing to work with evil, my evil, a task confronting humankind. Take a look around you at the mean, cruel aspect of life. Gratuitous cruelty, greed, injury. Why? We might as well be devils. Or, rather, we conceive of devils to give expression to the depth and reality of hate in us. Images of demons express how we feel, how we taste and look to ourselves in some way. Not entirely, not essentially, but importantly. Devils are part of poetry and poetry expresses and forms life. There is nothing more real than feelings to which poetry bears witness. Emotional imagination is real. Tillich sets an enormous task, a necessary vision. How will the human race work with its destructiveness?

Freud spoke of sublimation. Channelling, even transforming, instinctual life creatively. Transformational processes have long been part of spirituality. Yet, often, a model of taming and control is centre stage, controlling lower nature, taming it. Results often have been horrendous. Prisons, punishment, threats, rewards, wars, self-crippling, and the battery of mechanisms psychoanalysis charts, rerouting of what is "tamed", "controlled" in ways that overturn, break through, rebel. The wild within damages the controller.

Can we find a better model? Not control or idealised sublimation. Can we partner our capacities, work *with*, not just against them? Learn who we are, what we can do, what we are up against? Assimilate, digest, not just fight, push away, break. Let life in—how?

* * *

In my thirties. Writing. I should say, writing and writing and writing. I thought of people like Lawrence Durrell, who could write for weeks non-stop. Many writers could do that, write and write. For me, tension built, much too much tension. Red lines broke out on my neck and down my chest. It was impossible. The Vision—to give expression to—It, the Real Thing, Life—IT. The more I tried, the more I failed.

A few years later, I came across Merleau-Ponty's writing on Cezanne. Cezanne wanted to capture the snowiness of a tablecloth Balzac described. Try as he would to paint the snowiness evoked by Balzac's words, he failed. Finally, he gave up and just tried to paint a tablecloth. And there it was, snowiness and all.

Sometimes you have to give up on the thing itself, the real-most X, and do what you *can* do.

Two moments stand out. The first was a vision of mortality. Something like a voice told me that if I was to write, I had to accept mortality. The voice was my own being, a dream voice. It was *me*, perhaps a transcendent me, an inner guide. We have a guiding function that helps if we can tap it. This happened by itself, unsought, probably owing to the build-up of intensity of trying with all my might, trying too hard. It was a flash, a seeing, a felt realisation. My work would be imperfect. It would miss the thing itself, X, the Truly Real. It would be less than I wanted. To write, this had to be accepted, tolerated, admitted, like death. I would have to bear my work not being what I wanted it to be. I would have to live with it as it is, as it develops, warts and all. There was no way around this. To write, I had to be mortal. To pass through this tunnel, this veil. To simply be. To write, I would have to be a failure. A pain a writer, at least this writer, must live with. A releasing pain. The time was coming when I could stop throwing everything I wrote away. The time was coming when I could write because I failed.

The great surprise—like Cezanne and Balzac's snowiness—over the years, accepting or tolerating or living with necessary failure gave birth to moments I despaired of finding, moments of X, the real thing itself, truth and life and beauty, what I hoped for but gave up on. It came by itself through the doing, acceptance of what I could and could not do, mining openings.

* * *

Mining mortality was one thing, but the tension continued. I accepted, or was on the way to accepting, my plight as a writer, the most real would evade me. But I did not have a clue how to go about working with the tensions writing plunged me into. The more I wrote, the more tension mounted, and I was semi-oblivious to the pressure I was living. Then, one day, without quite knowing how, I found myself on a plane for Paris. Apparently, I could not take the intensity and something blew or perhaps almost blew, and my system's way of handling it was to fly to Paris. There I roamed the streets a little like Woody Allen's protagonist in *Midnight in Paris*. But I was not so lucky as to meet great authors and musicians of the 1920s. One thing about this trip: I wrote nothing and was lucky to make two French friends, male and female, who took me to their favourite places. I felt taken care of, nursed, nourished. The man kept saying *jouissance* left Paris, he was going to move to the country. Both said they could not believe I was American. They had a very different picture of "Americans".

The trip lasted longer than I expected. I went to Israel, Greece, Italy, then back to London, where I called R. D. Laing and D. W. Winnicott.

* * *

Laing did not have time to see me. I heard only the voice of a secretary. Winnicott picked up the phone himself. His "hullo" was cheering and we set a time. When I walked in the door, he shook my hand and greeted me saying, "Hullo, Dr Eigen. I'm sorry I haven't read your books." Well, I was just a struggling graduate student. No books, no articles. No doctor. I was having a hard time in school, although I got much from parts of it. Other parts were torture, what I called the slave stage, learning a foreign language I would never speak. It took eleven years to get my doctorate, going part time, working in schools, treatment centres, and clinics. I was no one he could or should know. Yet, to Winnicott I was special, Dr Eigen, writer of books he had not read and I had not written. What a lovely feeling he engendered.

He served sherry and as we spoke said, "Are you seeing Laing? So many want to see him now." He was curious why I was seeing him and not R. D. Laing. I could not say I called Laing first and he did not see me. He bantered along thoughtfully—thoughtful banter—saying, "We're worried about Laing. We're afraid fame will lead him to lose contact with clinical practice." By lose contact, he meant something more than not doing it. He meant something like doing it without the nitty-gritty.

Years later, I was consulted by a former Laing patient, although the word patient does not quite fit. Contact would be more like it—moments of significant contact. He had important moments with Laing, especially on LSD, but afterwards, when the high faded, Laing lost interest. He was not interested in the "working through", just the intense points. The slow, hard drudge of daily practice did not appeal. The man who consulted me got a lot from these "psychic hits", but was raw and dangling from lack of work in the trenches, the work that assimilates. This reminds me of a remark by Chogyam Trungpa in the 1960s. When a student complained of a boring place Trungpa picked to meditate, the latter said, "Boredom, exactly what you need." He was thinking of the "highs" and speed Americans were addicted to and thought boredom might help. Winnicott was prescient, not boring, but also had staying power.

I felt called upon to say something and said how much I liked his paper on manic–depressive tendencies, which, among other things, he likened to death and resurrection, up and down movements. He shrugged my praise off, saying, "Oh, that. I wrote it to enter the Society." I really did like it but had to take in the political intent that was part of it. I felt a little embarrassed but touched by his open practicality.

As we got into the visit, Winnicott seemed unconscious of time. It is difficult to pin down this feeling. I felt it with Bion, too. A loss of time consciousness. Just into the thing that was happening now, the present reality. It felt as if we had all the time in the world, our time together would never end. Now I think it was because it was always beginning. Both Winnicott and Bion were always beginning.

Winnicott was a mixture of stillness and quirky movement. He could sit still in compressed concentration and without warning, change positions, go to another part of the room. For a long time he sat at the edge of his therapy couch, screwed himself up, a corkscrew. He put a lot of physical strength into his thought, a thin man with kindly, electric tension. His face seemed female. Yet, an angular, masculine strength came through, too. I thought of Jung's remark about older women becoming more masculine and older men more feminine. I do not know how true Jung's remark is, but Winnicott combined both.

He was trying to find the best way to tell me something, to convey something to me about the way he worked. Not simply how he worked, but something about psychic reality. He wanted me to get a sense of something he felt important, searching to find a way to evoke in me a reality that was real to him. He had already made several attempts, but was not satisfied that I got it. My sense was that he was not dissatisfied with me, but with how he went about it. He was trying to communicate a significant area of experience that I was not locating. It took me a while to take in the realisation that from his point of view, I was missing it or it was missing me, that there was something in the room that did not find me. I thought I was following him and had no sense I was missing it (see Eigen & Govrin, 2007).

He seemed a little satisfied after telling me the following story. A woman he worked with was trying to centre his image in a hand mirror, while he was seated behind her. He bent over and could see his face slightly off centre, so moved to centre it. He knew immediately he had made an error. In the next session, she told him that had this happened six months earlier, she would be back in hospital. He had played the helpful mother who could not stand being off balance. Keeping his image off-centre was precisely what his patient was doing and he was unable to let it happen. He had to fix it, "right" it. His little story got through to me how important it is to tolerate off-balance states. Life is filled with them. Trying to tidy them up to maintain imaginary homeostasis clouds reality.

I thought of the case in Winnicott's (1953) transitional object paper, in which the child had to keep her mother in good repair, help her feel balanced. The child functioned as a kind of transitional object, keeping her mother in life. Her mother could not let the child's aliveness wax and wane. The mother's aliveness depended on her child's aliveness and loss of aliveness in the child meant loss of aliveness in the mother. It was quite a pressure, keeping oneself emotionally alive to stop mother's feeling from dying off.

Near the end of our meeting, Winnicott offered me books by Fairbairn, Guntrip, and himself. I had read Fairbairn and Guntrip, so he found another Guntrip I had not seen, published in London, *Healing the Sick Mind*. We spoke about Guntrip and Fairbairn and what he valued in them. One of the books he gave me was a collection of his BBC talks on mothers and babies, which I reread many times with melt-in-your-mouth pleasure.

He mentioned that he was considering an invitation to speak in New York and wondered how he would be received. He was concerned and worried. I was taken aback that he would ask me, so little equipped to tell him. It was near the end of August 1968. I said if they were like me, they would want to hear him, but I feared there was a wide mix of people in the field, many defensive and biased, and it depended whom he spoke to. Later, I learnt that he came to New York and spoke to an unreceptive, aggressive group, a meeting with a bad outcome. I wrote him once or twice afterwards and he wrote back, keeping things open, saying something like, "We'll see. We'll see."

I met Winnicott near the end of his life, his creativity in full bloom. I was left with a profound sense that if he could be him, I could be me. He was so himself, quirky, awkward, unapologetic about his intensity, that it freed me to be more myself. A deep kind of permission that if a sensibility like his could exist, then a sensibility like mine could, too. This may sound presumptuous, but it springs from his need to share his own sensibility, his sense of reality, a spontaneous striving.

* * *

After I came back to New York, I had a dream. I was painting large canvases. I am not sure, but there was a sense of frustration. The image changed and I was painting small pictures and was told I should paint small, not large, canvases. I awoke with a sense that I was trying to do too much and should pour myself into smaller frames. I was able to do a lot in smaller, more contained works, more able to distil intensity. With this as a guide, I was able to begin and finish papers, leading to my first psychoanalytic publications in 1973, five years after meeting Winnicott. Trying to do less, I found myself able to do more.

* * *

In 1977, at the age of forty-one, I met W. R. Bion. He gave a week of seminars in New York City under the auspices of the Institute for Psychoanalytic Training and Research. I attended the seminars, the party, the public lecture, and had two therapy sessions. I felt I was learning something, although I was not sure what.

It is hard to unpack the moment I walked into his hotel room for a session. A tall man, quickly adapting to my shorter height, making room. It is hard to define such moments of tact, they happen so quickly. I had a fleeting impression that he looked like a bug. Now, years later, I wonder, did I see my own buggy self? I could have felt threatened but, if I did, I also felt reassured. I felt here was someone I could try to talk to and began testing the waters. Did I see hints of fear? If so, that added to kinship across distance. We were such different people, from different ages. He had a kind of formality yet gracious, accepting, inviting. I thought of the word "under-stand", to stand under, to provide an emotional floor simply by being present. What did we share? Perhaps love of the psyche, the respect, caution, and risk this love requires.

We spoke of many things and at one point he said that ordinarily he would not say so much, but we had so little time. I wonder if he, too, felt something *simpatico*. I will tell you some of what I remember in the order it comes to me now, rather than strain to re-create the order in the sessions, which I doubt I can do. A quality of the flow involved things that seemed to come to him out of the blue. In his seminar talks, the only writer who had worked in America that he mentioned was Theodore Reik, particularly his *Surprise and the Psychoanalyst* (1936). Surprise with deep psycho-logic.

A theme that emerged was the difficulty involved in finding, being, creating one's self, the "nasty business" (his words) of being real. I spoke to him about difficulties I was having with a former supervisor who had been so helpful. Now, at meetings, he became abusive. After my publications started coming out, his attitude towards me changed. Actually, my publications affected my status in many ways at the clinic I worked in. The head of the clinic suddenly paid attention to me. When we discussed an issue, he would turn to me and say, "Let's see what Mike says." I can see how this aggravated my former supervisor. Bion spoke of difficulties with being an individual, perceiving differently. I had the feeling he was speaking from experience. He encouraged me to go my way and meet the difficulties this brought.

When he heard about my intricate relationship with a former analyst and the latter's unresolved influence on me, he felt I must break away, struggle with the nasty business of finding myself. He spoke of Rickman saving him from Klein. John Rickman was Bion's earlier analyst and had a wider, undogmatic, independent perspective. Bion gained from Klein's more narrow, deep view, but felt a need to retain autonomy, which his previous analysis supported. He had a keen appreciation for the struggle to be a person and felt him trying to support my struggle.

At one point I remarked, "You remind me of Marion Milner." He said, "A lot of people tell me that." I was thinking of ways each was concerned with self. I had met Milner three years earlier and was struck by a similarity. Perhaps no accident, too, that Winnicott, Milner, and Bion were, in their own ways, artists. In one of his last seminars, the Paris seminar, he spoke of the psychoanalyst as artist.

* * *

I told him a dream that involved a wild figure, something like King Kong, a gorilla in the jungle, it is vague now, but alive then. He must have felt I played it down in some way because he sided with the wild one and said, "You know, it's real." Meaning the dream, the emotional reality of the dream is real. He spoke of it being part of myself, then paused and corrected himself. "You know, we speak of parts, parts of yourself, but they're not parts. They're *you*." I immediately felt the wholeness of the fragmented dream experience, a wholeness of being in my fragmented states. Me, not parts of me. The dream figure that scared me was me myself. I scared myself. I am afraid of myself. I thought of the common expression, "It's only a dream," often used to reassure a child who lacks capacity to take in and assimilate the terror of the night, so intimately related to the terror of the day. I felt that both Bion and I shared this fear.

* * *

Out of the blue, Bion said, "Do you know the Kabbalah. The *Zohar*?" There was no warning or precedent for this remark that I knew of. Maybe his perception that I was Jewish. Several years later, I came across remarks in a Brazil seminar that showed Bion was conscious of "race": in one case, a Jewish individual who disowned, or was not aware of or rooted in, the richness of his background, a denial that characterised much in his life, not just his Jewishness. Was he testing the depths, my moorings? Did he pick something up about the realness of spiritual life for me? Was he touching a convergence between us I did not take in? How did he know religion was such an important part of my sensibility? Was it like the dream, he taking as real something I was afraid to value as much as I did? This was an emergent theme than ran through our disjointed, seemingly unrelated communications—he valuing what in myself I feared to fully value and fully live.

"Yes, I mean, well, not really, no, yes, " I replied. I read aspects of Kabbalah for many years. "I mean, I read the *Zohar* but don't really *know* it." I read intermittently, haphazardly, parts of *Zohar* and other writings over twenty years. He quickly replied, "Yes, likewise. I read it, but don't really *know* it." He paused, then added, "I use the Kabbalah as a framework for psychoanalysis." I was floored, motionless. It is a remark I am still mining.

By the time I met Bion, I had heard Joseph Campbell use the *chakras* and Hindu mythos as a framework for Freud and Jung. But Bion came to me within psychoanalysis itself. His remark blew open a shell and brought me to a new level of freedom. I cannot do justice to all the themes of our contacts, but freedom was one of them, going along with the realness of oneself, one's life. This past year or two, a member of my Bion–Winnicott–Lacan seminar invited me to give seminars on Kabbalah and Psychoanalysis (Eigen, 2012a) for the New York University Contemplative Studies Project. How he got to this, I do not know. It was not something I had in mind, but I can feel Bion's impact in the background.

* * *

The momentary awkward back and forth about "knowing" Kabbalah reminds me of Bion's end of sessions behaviour. He never told me the session was over. We kept talking and I began to wonder, was it up to me to end? As minutes ticked past the session time, I grew uncomfortable, and stood up. Neither of us hid a sort of semi-awkwardness, as if we were getting the feel of what to do moment to moment. He seemed in no rush, no rush at all. Likewise, payment. What would have happened if I had not asked? Would we still be sitting there today? Obviously not—but what is this mutual sensing, leaving it to me? Perhaps in an inner sense, we *are* still sitting there today, sensing, exploring, tasting.

* * *

In one of our meetings, I found myself talking about Rilke, who creates realities as he writes, creates new possibilities of sensibility as combinations of words are born. Someone told me that Rilke lacked humour. I found myself recycling this remark and blurted to Bion, "There's something joyless about you." It was as if I took in a foreign voice and spoke from it, funnelling a narrow vision of my own, perhaps demon me, fearful me. What faith must it take to be Rilke, opening worlds at the edge of what it is possible to experience, hearts of experience. Bion writes of faith in face of unknown emotional reality. Yet, I called him joyless. Was I saying what I saw, or defending against an experience our meetings were creating?

He responded, "Well, if joy is important to you, it must be in your body, your being, your skin." That is, if I was joyful, it cannot just be in my head. It has to be cellular, in my pores, enfleshed in my life, lived joy, not theory. It was a remark I have thought about for many years. It applies to much that we say. We can talk about feeling, but living feelings, experiencing experience, is another matter.

At the end of the IPTAR (Bion, 1980) seminars, Bion looked at me (did I imagine it?) and said something like, "Odd, how going through something as gruelling as this work can bring such joy."

* * *

Two of my girlfriends saw Bion for sessions, probably spurred by my seeing him. He had glimpses of me from other perspectives than mine. I spoke to him about difficulties with women. At one point, out of the blue, he said, "You should get married. Marriage is not what you think. It's someone you can speak truth to and help mitigate the severity to yourself."

Without expecting it, a whole deeper field of experience opened. Someone to speak truth to and help mitigate the severity to yourself. The words, the sentiment, cut through primitive fears, whatever they were—fear of engulfment, feeling trapped, being let down, abandoned, wounded beyond repair, unimaginable loss, fear of my own murderous rage, you name it.

I spoke about the women I was seeing and wondered whether I should seek someone new, seek a fresh start, my relationships were so blemished. He referred to a paper I gave him, published in the *International Journal of Psychoanalysis* (1977) "On working with 'unwanted' patients". It summarised ten years of clinic work with intractable dependency, wounded dependency, and, especially, hostile dependency. He said, if not laconically, in a low-keyed way, "Do you need more hostile dependent relationships?"

At some point he said, "Stop analysis. You've had enough analysis." It was time to live my life, not keep analysing it. The two are not incompatible, but he felt my tie to analytic work was keeping me from marriage, another kind of commitment. I picture jumping into oceans other than ones I knew. He touched a deep core and longing. I wanted to marry, to be a father, and ever since I can remember assumed this would happen. I worked with children as a young man and expected to get married and become a father in my twenties. I entered analysis instead. Contact with the living psyche took on a kind of priority, a lifelong work. Twenty years passed.

Someone else could have said what Bion said. My father might have said it. But Bion's voice carried weight, touched psychic reality, resonated. A mere stranger, but I could believe him. He spoke from a place I believed. He was not a girlfriend, not my parent. Perhaps he simply said what was true for him, his own emotional truth, which touched mine.

When I wrote my "unwanted patient" paper, I did not fully see I was addressing my own hostile dependency, wounded dependency, to be dependent and push or run away, intractably dependent and dependency phobic. But I was aware that Bion was giving me a compassionate push towards further development, another stage of life, one I almost slid past.

Later, I thought of Freud working from unconscious to unconscious and Bion from psychosis to psychosis. The fact that Bion so acutely touched faces of madness made his faith in living the more valuable to me. Facing the diabolic in oneself? Yes, but Bion went further (Bion, 1970; Eigen, 1998).

* * *

I wondered about the semi-oracular pronouncements Bion made—stop analysis, get married. Did he say the same thing to everyone? What did he tell my girlfriends? One with whom I was in a very painful–pleasurable in–out, hostile–dependent relationship, did he tell her to stop analysis and get married? He told her she had a father problem that would wreck a marriage. He told her not to get married but have more analysis. He had a more favourable response to the other woman. I wondered if he was blessing the latter relationship and advising against the former.

There was a third girlfriend he did not meet and, three years after seeing Bion, we married and started a family. How that happened is another story, worth telling, but not now. I became a father at the age of forty-five; my wife was thirty-six. To say everything changed is an understatement. Challenges I never dared face became imperative. If I wanted my marriage to work and my family to survive me, I would have to undertake a rapid rate of growth that psychically resembled something like the rate of physical growth an embryo-foetus undergoes. Life was beginning in new ways that made the previous decade almost look like a standstill.

Similarly, my practice. I always tried my best with patients and all aspects of my work. But to begin to feel towards them a sense of care that paralleled aspects of what I felt towards my children brought new affective resonance, new spirit. I was the same old me, limitations, warts and all, the failures patients have to put up with if they stay with me. Even so, other dimensions of care and possibilities opened, hard to define, but real. You cannot give what you cannot access. Bion, I feel, supported me in accessing more.

* * *

I would like to mention a few odds and ends relating to Bion's visit to New York in 1977. At the party, I was one of those who stood around him as he recited passages from Milton's *Paradise Lost*. My father used to recite Milton's "L'Allegro" and "Il Pensoroso" and tell me what they meant. Both Bion and my father appreciated poetry. Heine was my father's favourite poet.

You might find it odd to see a renowned eighty-something psychoanalyst at a party reciting Milton's *Paradise Lost*. All kinds of thoughts raced through my head—does he have difficulty relating? Is he autistic? Schizoid? Yet, the fuller message was: he was being himself, his idiosyncratic self. As with Winnicott, a message came through: if he could be Bion, I could be me. Seeing him recite Milton at a New York social gathering made me feel freer to be me.

In his public lecture, he spoke of being in a tank that shook like jelly. Metal turns to jelly. He spoke of fear in battle and fear in analytic sessions. He gave the impression that with no fear, you are out of contact with reality. Without fear, you are out of contact with the session. He felt they decorated him wrongly for bravery in action; he was a frightened soldier who got the idea that you can get killed running away from the enemy as easily as going towards him. Hearing him speak, being with him, I had no sense that he was going to die the next year. His last year was filled with seminars, reaching others, sharing whatever he had, stimulating growth.

As he spoke, I thought of our two sessions. He was encouraging me to move towards life, my life. The metal that surrounded me like skin shook like jelly. To be afraid is part of living in reality. What one makes of it is something else.

CHAPTER THREE

On Winnicott

Winnicott is one of those men who changed my life. I would like to share with you some of the writings that helped me. I have written elsewhere of my meeting with him in 1968, before he spoke in New York (Eigen & Govrin, 2007). I began reading Winnicott in the 1960s and he is one of the few analytic writers I have continued to read closely for sustenance, inspiration, and learning. Over forty years of reading Winnicott, and not a sign of being tired of him. On the contrary, like reading Rilke, his words open realities, create or discover realities.

There is much in his work I am leaving out: transitional experiencing, illusion–disillusion, paradox, play, psyche–soma, vital spark, incommunicado core, unaliveness, being alone together, unintegration, fear of breakdown, creativity, to name a few. At another time, another mood, I might have chosen any of them, or others, to write on. The present communication focuses on three areas that teach me much about clinical work and living as I grow older, now the same age as Winnicott when he died. The more I dwell with them, the deeper they go: writings on use of the object, aloneness, and madness.

Before jumping in, I would like to comment on a particular atmospheric background of his work. Perhaps it is my temperament or sensibility, but, very early in my reading of Winnicott, I felt a sense of relief. As I looked closely at this relief, one of the ingredients I noticed was a lack of contempt for dependency in his work. This was rare in my experience up to that point. I felt a certain judgemental, even moralistic quality when it came to "regression", "pre-oedipal", "paranoid–schizoid" tendencies. Emphasis was on "making the oedipal", "making the depressive position", with a kind of shame attached to "inferior" levels of development. I could breathe more freely with Winnicott, with myself, with my patients, more readily take people as they are without demeaning judgements, stay with what is, opening fields of experience.

Use of object

I long felt that Winnicott's (1969) use of object formulation constitutes a breakthrough in psychic evolution. His vision sets a challenge, provides a basis for meditation and reverie, not only food for thought, but a new sense of the real. He speaks of "destructive" aliveness as "a symptom of being alive" and not "anger at the frustrations that belong to meeting the reality principle" (1992, p. 239). This reminds me of Freud before the death drive, when aggression was part of Eros (Winnicott writes, "at the start aggressive drives are associated with muscle erotism and not with anger or hate"). For Freud, hate played a very early role in response to reality, at once an attack on a frustrating situation, an attempt to evade, escape, tone down painful stimuli, perhaps an attack on frustration tied to incapacity to tolerate build-up of experience.

It is possible to envision early hate of frustration/frustrating reality as a kind of destruction of the latter, a wish or attempt to destroy and rid oneself of too much or feared disturbance. Let us say the baby's scream at this moment is part of an explosion that blindly aims to blot out or destroy the pain of life. Such an event is reflected in self and world destruction experiences, images, narratives in psychosis, severe trauma, and cosmic myths.

Winnicott adds to this the possibility of a constitutive, not simply reactive, destruction. Not only reactive hate trying to blot out frustration, but a more primordial destruction that is part of the rhythm of life. He likens it to breathing, "the first and subsequent breaths, out-breathing" and uses the fire of dragon breath as an image, quoting Pliny, "Who can say whether in essence fire is constructive or destructive?" (1992, p. 239).

Let me exaggerate to bring home what I feel is a very real experience, a nuclear experience, a basic rhythm: world destruction followed by world survival. The world is destroyed. The world survives. Life is destroyed. Life survives. The object is destroyed. The object survives. Bion (Eigen, 2004, pp. 27–36) adds to this the experience of being murdered and being all right, a new twist to an ancient theme.

Freud suggested that in psychosis a destroyed object world can be reconstituted in an hallucinatory key. In the Schreber case, he describes a blackout, world destruction, followed by the world miracled up, regained through a hallucinatory prism. Winnicott turns this around, and presto—the world that was the object of destruction survives the latter and, in so doing, becomes more real. It is a different moment. My destruction is creative. It is the opposite of Fairbairn saying that the schizophrenic feels his love is bad. There is a way Fairbairn, I suspect, is right: my love is bad, my love destroys—a very real state. But Winnicott touches another nerve: my destructive force is creative because You survive it. The fate of my primordial destructive force hinges on the nature of environmental responsiveness, a destruction that creates/discovers reality anew because of the latter's capacity to respond—a new turn on the creative destruction theme.

How does this happen? Winnicott's depiction has many threads, one involving the fullness of the infant's emotion meeting the mother's ability to survive it without caving in or retaliating. In this case, reality not only survives destruction, but survives it well. Surviving the baby's emotive force with intact presence creates a sense of world that can survive emotion and be used for emotional growth.

Winnicott is not saying that frustration–hate or guilt–reparation do not exist. They are real and play important roles in development all through life. He is pointing to another state in which all-out emotion meets a more or less whole response, a sense that the world is not destroyed by feeling but sustains the latter's development. The world survives me and can take my need to use it for emotional development. The other's capacity to survive makes it usable.

Another way of putting this: feelings have a place in the world. It is, at least some of the time, a world that can take expression of feeling and support evolution of feeling. Picture the opposite, a situation in which feelings are experienced as damaging and must be controlled, sat on, blotted out, evaded—a world that cannot take feelings, or cannot take them well. A world we find ourselves in or up against much of the time. Both states, the one Winnicott is reaching and the more usual control or evasion models, are part of being human.

Winnicott is trying to address destructiveness in a new way, not simply with a "control" or "reparation" model. He seeks a moment in which destruction plays a creative role in constituting a world outside me, one that can be used for my development because it can survive or "take" my development. I have called this a joy based model (Eigen, 1981a), but it is more than joy, although delight, surprise, amazement may be part of awakening to the realness of reality, an emergent sense of the real: reality can be all this! Perhaps one can say there is a sense of being real, of realness, and that Winnicott touches a sense of the realness of realness. It is a moment in which destructiveness does not have to be controlled or atoned for, but can breathe, enter into feeling communion, and further creation/discovery of feeling.

One of the great problems in development is our need to shut off feeling and inhibit movement in order to control destructive urges. Winnicott is trying to find a way to give destruction its due, precisely because the environment survives and is newly envisioned. Instead of a destroyed world being reconstituted as hallucination in order maintain object contact, the world opens to a fuller dimension of being, rooted in capacity to contain, absorb, and work with feeling. Can we survive our feelings and survive them well? Winnicott here responds affirmatively.

He writes of adolescence: "the good is not that which is handed down by parental benignity but that which is forced into being by individual adolescent destructiveness" (1992, p. 239). A good that becomes real and serviceable because it can withstand attacks. How practical is this in real life? I am not too good at survival in the moment, but come back, reconstitute over time. I need to extend Winnicott's description to depict process over time, sometimes in the same session, sometimes a week, sometimes months. Over time, I do come back, find a path towards better contact and sustenance. There are times in sessions that I might admit being done in, even say, "You killed me, but not forever." Part of what sessions are about is whether we can survive each other and with what quality. Add to that, whether and how one survives oneself.

One reason Winnicott does not emphasise a death drive is because the life drive wreaks enough havoc. An important theme: can life survive itself? Life itself has destructive tendencies—territoriality, possessiveness, the assertion of me over you, not just survival but domination, triumph, lust for power. We kill to live. We do not have to go to a death drive to see how life-affirming tendencies destroy life. We do not know what to do with the destructive force of our life drive, let alone a death drive. Destructiveness is part of pleasure, exercise of elan, vitality. Aliveness destroys; aliveness is dangerous. We do not know what to do with our aliveness. Jesus brings this out: Father, forgive them, they don't know what they're doing. And, indeed, we do not.

Winnicott envisions a moment that offers another possibility, a way to experience maximum emotion, especially destructiveness, which, if met well, opens new possibilities of living. He claims this is a real possibility, to which his work bears witness. Yet, even if it were only a vision, it opens new doors of development.

A strange world we live in where a central theme is: can the mother take the baby's aliveness and with what quality? Can we survive each other's aliveness? Can we survive our own aliveness and how? The fate of feeling depends on capacity to respond to it, an evolutionary challenge. This highlights a circle. Where does capacity to respond to the infant's destructive force come from? From having been responded to as an infant? A basic issue is how do we create/discover conditions to support our capacity to respond? The spotlight is on mixtures of capacity–incapacity and problems that, one way or another, we share.

There are many processes that go into making a sense of the real. In other contexts, Winnicott notes that the environment can fail by adapting too much or too little, too much illusion or disillusion. Life is made of mixtures. As Leonard Cohen sings, "There's a crack in everything; that's how the light gets in". Failure is part of growth. We need to learn how not to be with each other in order to learn to be together. So many processes go into give and take. What I have called reparation, control, and need-frustration models are parts of the pool. I am leaving such qualifying and necessary aspects of psychic life aside to bring out a moment Winnicott creates/discovers that can be missed. Yet, finding it is like coming upon an Archimedean point that makes a profound difference in how it feels to be alive, another way of experiencing inner–outer reality, another approach.

Another of the threads that can be picked in Winnicott's use of object discussion is the co-emergence or separation of "fantasy and actual placing of the object outside the area of projections" (1992, p. 239). He writes of an unconscious backcloth in which destructive fantasies go on while the object (reality) survives outside them. You might think the subject is disappointed that the object survives, that survival of the other amounts to frustration of destructive impulses or intentions. This can be the case and, in certain circumstances, often is. But that is not the state at issue here. Winnicott touches a moment in which survival of the other brings relief. Not only relief, but a sense of realness of a living world, made more real by the backcloth of destructive fantasy it survives.

Winnicott envisions an area of experience in which maximum destruction in fantasy keeps our sense of reality fresh. It is a different alternative to the monster within, guilt, horror at one's make-up, and efforts at control alternating with breakdown of control, important as all these are. It makes for greater possibilities of play and seriousness, appreciation and use of otherness, in which, paradoxically, destruction affirms difference and difference affirms destruction. It opens experiencing to new dimensions and further explorations.

I would like to end this section on use of object with a letter I received from Clare Winnicott, soon after my paper, "The area of faith in Winnicott, Lacan and Bion" (1981a) was published. It was the first paper to call attention to the importance of Winnicott's use of object formulation and to bring out some of its implications. At the time, I thought it the climax of his work, but now, after another thirty years of reading Winnicott, I feel there may have been a number of "climaxes". Clare Winnicott writes of it in terms of their life together, an important ingredient in how they lived.

> Dear Dr. Eigen,
>
> Some time ago you told me that a paper of yours discussing the work of D.W. and Bion in relation to each other was to come out in the International. I have now read the paper, and I must say how delighted and relieved I was to find that at last someone had really understood the "Use of an Object" paper, and seen it as an idea that revitalises basic living and gives it another dimension.
>
> I know that for Donald this was the climax of his theoretical formulations – the place that he had been seeking to arrive at. And I think this

can be seen in his previous work as one thing led to another. The "Use of an Object" paper was in a sense his final word, his resting place, although of course he was planning to write more, and to develop ideas around transitional experience and phenomena.

I remember one summer Sunday evening when Donald read the "Object" paper which he had been working on all day and had just finished – he read it to me for the first time after dinner. My response was total, and I knew that he had said something complete for himself which he had been working up to all his life. He had also said something about *us* and the way we lived. A mememtous [sic] evening.

Forgive me if I write only of Donald's paper, but I did also appreciate what you wrote about Lacan and Bion. I am more familiar with Bion, and can see links and differences more easily, and I am so glad you let them each be themselves and did not have to "harmonise their ideas" – as so many seem to have to do.

I would very much appreciate some off-prints of your paper.

Did you by any chance read what I wrote about Donald in Grolnick's book "Between Fantasy [sic] and Reality?" It was a first and painful effort, long ago now.

Thank you again for your very enjoyable, erudite and comprehensive paper on three creative people.

Yours sincerely,

Mrs. Clare Winnicott.

Aloneness

It might sound odd to think how much importance Winnicott placed on aloneness, given his emphasis on mother–baby interweaving. Yet, aloneness and an *incommunicado* core were basic to his sensibility and vision. It could be tempting to relate it to a thread of quietism in his Wesleyan background. He was the first, and nearly only, analyst I read who emphasised the importance of quiet states and even, at times, felt they were more basic than active excited states (for Freud, libido was basically active). I have amplified these themes elsewhere (1986, 2009, 2010, 2011a,b) and will focus mainly on one of his contributions, which I suspect is particularly his own, at least the tenor and feel of it.

Perhaps what is most moving and paradoxical about his account is that the quality and possibility of good enough aloneness is made possible by support the infant does not know it has. Winnicott writes of essential aloneness made possible by unknown support. The unknown support is mainly the infant's mother or primary care-taker, but the total environment and unknown world is part of it. An important piece of the experience and state of affairs Winnicott touches is that the baby receives support for its aloneness that it does not know is there.

> At the start is an essential aloneness. At the same time this aloneness can only take place under maximum conditions of dependence.
>
> Throughout the life of the individual there continues a fundamental unalterable and inherent aloneness, along with which goes unawareness of the conditions that are essential to the state of aloneness. (1988, p. 132)

This is a radical instance of his emphasis on the environment in supporting or failing emotional development. In his use of object account, the response of the environment was crucial for the very feel and psychic existence of an outside world, partly a containing outsideness, leading to difference between outside reality and unconscious backcloth of fantasy. In his account of aloneness, environmental support is linked with the biography of aloneness, whether and how and with what quality essential aloneness and capacity to be alone can survive and thrive. Consequences of wounded aloneness can be profound. In a recent work (2011b), I related wounded aloneness to addiction and showed the role therapy can play as the background support aloneness missed.

In *Human Nature* (1988), Winnicott has simple diagrams suggesting intricate moment-to-moment variations of emotional qualities of mother–infant interaction. He particularly emphasises how the mother's emotional states have immediate reverberations in the infant's, although the field is bi-directional. The very essence of aloneness is affected by what support and response it meets.

Just a note on the value he places on quietude:

> There was an unexcited state that was disturbed by the excited one, and deserves study in its own right. (1988, p. 114)

These excited experiences take place against a background of quietude, in which there is another kind of relationship between the baby and the mother. We are concerned with an infant in a highly dependent state and totally unaware of its dependence. (1988, pp. 101–102)

Sometimes, I describe a particular quality of quiet, perhaps part of *incommunicado* core, as a sabbath point of soul. Rather than holy frenzy, holy peace at moments and as an unfolding capacity. I also take liberties with Winnicott's formulation, staying true to my own sense of it, experiencing unknown background support as infinite, a background aura of infinite support. (Bion: "The fundamental reality is 'infinity', the unknown, the situation for which there is no language – not even one borrowed by the artist or the religious – which gets anywhere near to describing it" (1994, p. 372).)

Meditating on Winnicott's sense of aloneness, I once wrote,

> An aloneness that is supported by another one does not know is there. A primary aloneness, supported by an unknown boundless other. To think that aloneness has in its very core a sense of unknown infinite other. No wonder Winnicott says so much depends on the quality of environmental being and response. The very quality of aloneness depends on it.
>
> I, personally, experience something sacred in this core. I think Winnicott also did. Our lives tap into a sense of holiness connected with a background aura of infinite unknown support. That such an implicit sense is there offers no guarantees about how we use it. When the support basic aloneness needs cracks, vanishes, or is threatened, emergent self-feeling veers towards cataclysm. (2009, p. 12)

Winnicott also writes of being alone together, a thread of experience from infancy on. Shared aloneness, a valued state of being, in which there is sharing in the aloneness and aloneness in the sharing. In such states, we sense the background support Winnicott touches and value what it brings us.

Madness

The term "madness" is a familiar one in Winnicott's work. I suspect it has as a background ways in which the human race always felt it was mad. Melanie Klein, an important influence, focused on psychotic dynamics connected with destructive urges (Eigen, 1996, 2006a, 2010). Winnicott often "rewrote" aspects of Freud and Klein in his own way, his own emphasis, tone, and touch. In *The Psychotic Core* (1986), I show that concern with psychosis that is implicit near the beginning of psychoanalysis came out of the closet, blossomed fully, with such workers as Klein, Winnicott, Bion, Fairbairn, and Milner.

My focus here is Winnicott's later work on madness, which he sees as a centre of treatment. He writes of a conflict "between the fear of madness and the need to be mad" (1992, p. 126). For some individuals, relief and fuller growth occurs only by reaching an area of breakdown with roots early in life. Defences are organised around a sensed breakdown that could not be worked with when it happened, owing to incapacity. Yet, fear of breakdown continues and plays a role in a person's defensive needs. He describes a breakdown when personality begins to form, which, I suspect, can leave one frightened of beginnings. He writes, "cure only comes if the patient reaches to the original breakdown" (1992, p. 126).

Over time, the patient builds tolerance for anxiety states that were "unthinkable in their original setting". But it is not unusual to close up the moment the threat of madness is felt. He envisions an "original madness" or later "breakdown of defences" as unbearable. In therapy, the patient has a chance of reaching towards them, dipping in and out, building more tolerance. He calls the original, unbearable state of affairs X (I tend to re-write it as madness X; see my chapter, "Shadows of agony X" in *Toxic Nourishment*, 1999, where I also elaborate on Winnicott's hyacinth bulb image of the unlocalisable "scent" of madness). He writes, "What is absolutely personal to the individual is X". The very madness that terrifies us and that we escape from is also what feels most personal.

Making statements like this might sound too absolute. In Winnicott's work, such statements are qualified by many other considerations. Yet, dramatic statements call attention to important processes, points of emphasis. What is absolutely personal to the individual is his or her own madness that cannot be experienced. Winnicott posits breakdown states too unbearable to be fully experienced while they are happening or after they happened. Neither can they be remembered, because equipment to cognise them was not available.

Breakdown occurred before capacity to process it was developed. We read early breakdown states from tea-leaves of current anxieties. Yet, these leaves open paths to fuller experience. Winnicott writes,

> The continuation of the analysis means that the patient continually reaches to new experiences in the direction towards X and in the way I have described these experiences cannot be recalled as memories. They have to be lived in the transference relationship and they appear clinically as localised madnesses. (1992, p. 128)

Here is not only, or mainly, a matter of interpreting or "correcting" delusions, but of living through something or, in my experience, going through something together. In the course of failures of support or other mishaps in sessions, states that veer towards catastrophe spontaneously arise and, with help, one comes through them. This is work along a trauma–recovery continuum. Traumas of sessions precipitate partial "breakdowns" which carry with them hints of "original" breakdown, madness X. Part of the main work here is going through this together, coming through a difficult experience, offshoots of basic breakdown. What is lived through and gradually established is a rhythm of breakdown–recovery that I call a rhythm of faith. Faith that, when beset by cataclysmic dreads, one can, in time, come through. For this, as with use of object and primary aloneness, quality of support is essential.

In use of object, I learn the world survives me. In going through madness X, I learn that I can survive myself, I can survive my own psyche. Although failure of early support may have played a role in breakdown, it is me myself who is left to deal with its repercussions and see what I can and cannot do with it. I suspect breakdown is an inevitable part of experiencing, exacerbated or relieved by environmental complexities. In therapeutic work that Winnicott describes, I have a chance to live through breakdown, tap madness, go into these waters, because another who experiences going through it is with me, madness–recovery as repeatedly lived experience. Winnicott emphasises the importance of spontaneous recovery in sessions. The therapist functions as a kind of holding environment, creating an emotional atmosphere that facilitates coming through. Yet, specific qualities of the therapist and therapy relationship, a sense of the therapist's own ability–disability to come through, play a role. A paradoxical offshoot, I find, involves living through mixtures of shared madness, shared aloneness, shared recovery, *incommunicado* core to *incommunicado* core, uniquely one's own.

It is madness with a thousand faces, making its appearance in many ways and activities, in sessions, in politics, in culture. In one variation (1992, pp. 115–118; Eigen, 2002, pp. 151–155), Winnicott relates a patient's psychosomatic symptoms to dissociated madness, partly manifesting in sessions as a scream that was not screamed or experienced. Winnicott called the scream that was not experienced the "great non-event of every session". The session was a scream not known or felt explicitly, a scream partly linked with crying not met when the patient was a child: "the child cried and the mother did not appear". Winnicott suggests the scream his patient "is looking for *is the last scream just before hope was abandoned*. Since then screaming has been of no use because it fails in its purpose". His patient's scream made its appearance in a dream, breaking through the non-scream state, opening more possibilities of psychosomatic connection. Therapy atmosphere and dreaming interwove, creating new modes of contact.

When I met Winnicott in 1968, he told me of a patient trying to centre the image of his face in her hand-held mirror. He was seated behind her and could see his face was off centre in the mirror and moved to centre it. The moment he did that, he realised his error. In the next session she told him, "If you had done that six months ago, I'd be back in hospital." It was, in part, her mother's inability to tolerate not being the centre of her child's life that drove her child crazy. It was precisely the analyst's capacity to tolerate being off balance and off centre that the patient needed. The mother tried to use her child to create a false homeostasis, plug the leaks of her psyche, and perforated her child's psyche in the process. The session he told me also demonstrates progress in their work, his patient's growing ability not to be sunk by her analyst's "mistakes". In this case, she recovered between sessions. A common ground of cutting each other slack for being human was growing. Therapy provides practice in turning what could have been catastrophic interactions at one time into something workable, practice in spontaneous recovery.

A note on destruction

It seems paradoxical that Winnicott, who affirms a basic creativeness, wrote so much about destructiveness. He incorporated Freud's and

Klein's (Eigen, 1996, 2006a, 2010, 2011a,b) elaborations of destructive tendencies, but felt a need to rework them into a vision of his own. They remained important parts of psychic reality, but he felt something more was needed.

The work of destructive tendencies and conflict with them help to fuel madness. How can one meet destructive feelings without destroying feeling? Winnicott tried to find language for ways that emotional destruction can meet a saving response, part of the creative struggle to reach a good vein. In our time, the question of whether we can survive our destructive tendency is ever more urgent. As noted earlier, part of the difficulty is that destruction is a way of affirming life, part of life tendencies, part of aliveness. Winnicott tries to explore new ways of relating to destructive experience and its potential to contribute to overall growth and a growing sense of reality.

Based on his and Bion's work, it becomes possible to conceive sessions, in part, as practice in surviving mutual murder. I kill you; you kill me. We survive—or not. We survive partially and do not survive partially. We come through a session in better and worse ways. Coming through is always partly aborted. But that does not nullify it entirely. The story of Jesus is a depiction of coming through fully, murdered, abandoned, resurrected, supported. We go through the sequence in relative ways, while conceiving an absolute going through that Jesus models.

Practice in psychic destruction is freeing, if one "catches on" to the sequence, murder–survival, linked with resilience and responsiveness. Literal murder stops the process, a premature closure. It ends the possibility of letting experience build. What is at stake is the capacity to experience, to be partners with one's capacity to enable experience to develop. The destruction–responsiveness Winnicott speaks of are psychic events, parts of psychic processes. We need to develop the kind of psyche that can experience its destructive urges as expressions of living reality, potentially bringing new forms of intimacy and use of feeling interchange.

I think of the story of the thief and the Zen master. Townspeople catch the thief and bring him to the Zen master. The Zen master tells them, "Tie him in a halter suspended from a tree branch, taking care he does not get hurt and is as comfortable as possible in such a situation. Then bring him everything he wants". His thief-ness presumably grew out of deprivation and a feeling that if he is to get anything from life, he must get it himself—expect nothing from others. Dangling from a tree and being brought food or whatever is needed creates another paradigm, configuring his plight, making explicit a dependent dimension.

Another example of creative response to semi-dismissed need is Otto Weininger's (1996) report of a deprived, acting out child hungering for sweet cakes. Dr Weininger took him to a bakery and bought twenty-five or more cakes and let the boy eat as many as he wanted, an inconceivable happening bringing a new taste of life.

I am not suggesting these are Winnicottian moments, but they are questing attempts to loosen knots that are strangling aspects of human need. Similarly, there are many ways to go crazy and recover in sessions, a kind of thawing out of personality. Each therapy couple finds its own paths toward developing the capacity of coming through: coming through destruction, aloneness, madness, and much more. So much of this work has to do with sensing, including a sense of psychic support that helps wounded capacities in unsuspected ways.

CHAPTER FOUR

Winnicott: an added note

There is so much to dip into and explore. With Winnicott, I get the feeling that, deep as we go, there is more awaiting us. I am moved by a sense of "primary maternal preoccupation" as a thread of existence all life long. The older I get, the more important, rich, and full this capacity becomes, related as it is to devotion, sincerity, and care. I think, too, of variations of this capacity in Meltzer (1994) and Bion's (1994) concern with truth and life.

One thing one gets in psychoanalysis in general, and Winnicott in his own special way, is a sense of the interplay of psychic threads, always multiplicity. Bion speaks of sincerity as a "minimum necessary condition" (1994, p. 367) for "initiation" to a journey he values, while contrasting it with ways love becomes murderous, hate cruel, and the journey artificial. Even truth can become artificial. An echo of true–false reverberates through Winnicott's and Bion's writings.

True can be false and false true, partly depending on how a capacity is used or functions in a particular context. Winnicott depicts psychosis as taking the unreal as real and the antisocial tendency as making the untrue true (denial of dependency).

Twinships populate psychoanalysis. Ego–id, symmetrical–asymmetrical, exhibitionism–voyeurism, sadism–masochism, true–false selves, omnipotence–helplessness (Freud, Bion), omnipotence–need (Winnicott), absolute and relative truth and love, the list continues. The capacities, tendencies, and states alluded to enter varied relationships to one another. They can be antagonistic, fused, reversible, oscillating, symbiotic, co-nourishing, connected and distinguished in a variety of ways. Freud and Bion speak of basic binaries indistinguishable at an early point of origin. Bion elaborates the last as O, unknown, infinite, ultimate reality, in psychoanalysis, emotional reality. In one Bion diagram, O gives rise to "root", which gives rise to differentiated dimensions that characterise experience (1994, p. 323).

Winnicott, I feel, returns repeatedly to a "root" sense of life, how it feels to be alive, the taste of life. His work is a series of attempts to give expression to this unfolding "root" sense. In a nexus of attempts, he opens a dimension he calls "between", echoing Buber. Not just inner–outer, but between inner–outer. A transitional area, in one of its aspects an area of illusion, a kind of illusion that helps enrich life. This is a beautiful variation of the ancient theme of going beyond opposites. Since antiquity, there has been emphasis on balance between extremes, harmonising opposites, meeting of extremes, yin in yang and yang in yin. Aspects of Kabbalah teach that the middle way is not just a bland balance: something new is created (Eigen, 2012a).

This something new, I feel, runs through Winnicott's work. It is akin to, although not simply identical with, metaphor, where two terms enter a relationship opening vision or reality neither alone could reach. Transitional experiencing between baby and mother, between you and me, between writer and writing, between writing and reading, between . . . Not ownership or control, although these can enter (possessiveness of teddy bear). One can try to hold on to what one has found. But as one grows, one catches on that staying with an unfolding dimension can change one, enrich one, open experiential possibilities one needed but did not know existed. Where "between" can take us is largely unknown. I suspect it has international as well as familial implications.

William Blake's lines, "Eternity", which Marion Milner liked, emphasise one's relationship to experience. They seem more orientated to the experiencing subject, but implicitly express a "between" aspect in the subject's relationship to experience:

> He who binds to himself a joy
> Does the winged life destroy.
> But he who kisses the joy as it flies
> Lives in Eternity's sunrise.

Now I wish to emphasise a darker side. The destruction Blake mentions is a crucial thread in life. Winnicott felt a destructive tendency to be inherent in life: "At the present time I find I need to assume that there is a primary aggressive and destructive impulse that is indistinguishable from instinctual love appropriate to the very early stage of development" (1988, p. 79). Winnicott felt oral sadism to be a core clinical issue. The existence of this tendency is not due to environmental failure, but its development has some dependence on how it is met. It may be exacerbated or modulated by care received, but will never be fully transformed or nullified. We are mixed beings from the beginning and remain so all life long.

It is instructive to reflect on Guntrip's (1975) critique of his analysis with Winnicott. He felt that Winnicott's attempts to help him contact his aggression somehow missed the mark. He valued Winnicott's enabling presence and capacity to stay with and acknowledge deep trauma and emptiness and positive aspects of Guntrip's life. Guntrip's view was that if there was perfect mothering, there would be no aggression. In contrast, Winnicott looked for oral sadism near the beginning, partly associated with hunger. Critics of Guntrip's analysis with Winnicott felt Winnicott was too nice, unable to elicit or bear aggression. I found this a little puzzling, given his repeated tries to find it. Perhaps some aggression was expressed in Guntrip's critique? Guntrip felt Winnicott was not Winncottian enough (Eigen, 1981b), a kind of purist view of perfect mothering, beating Winnicott at his own game, as Guntrip conceived it. Winnicott felt that in healthy real life there are mixtures of tendencies, neither too nice or too nasty, but not without either. Whatever the "lack" in Guntrip's analysis, I felt a positive sense of shared values and vision enabled enough to happen to make it more than worthwhile—and a gift to us.

I would like to move towards closing by emphasising the mixed nature of life, something everybody knows. Freud spoke of "cure" partly being a matter of "quantity" tipping the balance towards life and the good (quantity begets quality). We are not ideal analysts or people and have mixed effects on ourselves and others and *vice versa*.

We are multi-dimensional, complex, positive, and negative. No one has solved the problem of human destructiveness, but many try to make things better. Freud, Klein, Bion, and Winnicott try to address core issues related to destructiveness in complex ways. They circle around the target, opening possibilities. Personally, I am a Freudian, Kleinian, Winnicottian, Kohutian baby and carry the influence of many others as well. Body work has been invaluable since my twenties. For me, psychoanalysis breathes. I am a psychoanalytic person. Whether or not I am a psychoanalyst, I dare not say. I find something of the O of psychoanalysis alive in me and that has made a difference. Thinking of Winnicott's extensions or openings, a psychoanalysis is what a psychoanalyst does.

One more note. Bion writes,

> The real nature of psychoanalytic methodology has never been properly assessed; there is a danger that the successes of the movement will be attributed to the ability of its students to apply conventional scientific method . . . rather than to the intuitive flair that made it possible for Freud at least to do more. (1994, pp. 238–239)

Winnicott, in his way, had a sense, a gift, a feel for opening dimensions of experience that add to life—a gift, I suspect, that may not have been so fully realised without the psychoanalytic setting, as the latter grows in possibilities with his touch.

CHAPTER FIVE

What is evil?

What is evil? It is a little like Pontius Pilate saying, "What is truth?" Where does one go to find a definition that would set what is truly evil off from bad things that happen? Much destruction goes on in life. Two great wishes of humankind are that there should be no evil or death.

No evil or death. We are partly defined by a capacity to wish the impossible. To wish the impossible and somewhere feel it might be possible. When Freud claimed there is no "no" in the unconscious, he might have meant we are the kind of creatures that believe the impossible is possible. More, that it is real. The impossible is real now—and this sense informs the feel of reality. And when reality does not conform to our vision of bliss, we may call it evil.

What does reality want of us? One answer is absolutely nothing. A terrifying answer. Shakespeare suggested we live a masquerade within which is nothing. A relief? Does nothing free us from evil spectres? Or clear a way for them?

When I was a child, I saw the opening of the concentration camps in film newsreels. People who looked like death, whose eyes glared in ways that only eyes that have seen evil can. The scene switches to mass graves, naked bodies piled upon one another, macabre sandwiches in dirt. Horrific death scenes that added meat to my already burgeoning terrors of witches, devils, and the night. Yet, when I was older, I could not stop myself from picturing what it must be like to be inside Hitler. Past the psychopath, the killer, the madman, the calculus of hate and power and revenge, into pain, the torment of the human. Blistering wounds that sought healing in inhuman madness, nests of megalomanic hate. What pain and torment must have festered there. Pain made visible by horror inflicted on others. From the outside, evil, yet, further inside, deeper seas of pain.

Evil from the outside, pain from the inside. I think of a short story by Graham Greene about a man who kills a young woman just as he begins to feel something for her, just as her presence began to touch him. What is it that is so afraid that it needs to kill the capacity to be touched?

To kill off feeling—a crucial vector in human life. And, for some of us, the awful things we do to bring some feeling back.

Freud, Klein, and Bion write of a destructive force within (Eigen, 1998, 2010). In *The Psychotic Core* (1986) I write of Freud shifting the discourse from sin to madness. Yet, it was not new to call evil mad. Terms like madness and folly were in cultural discourse, referring to crazy, evil, foolish things we do, spectrums of possibility. God was referred to not only as the Great Musician, but the Great Physician, whose care was to cure souls. But Freud took Shakespeare to heart, that human ills came not from the stars but from within. Psychology of human beings was front and centre stage. A psychology of the soul, of personality. Again, nothing entirely new, but an emphasis opening doors, an Archimedean shift of leverage.

If the Pentateuch ends with the question of whether we will choose good or evil, Freud ends with the question of whether we will choose life or death. Biblically, evil, sin was associated with death. I suspect some idea or sense of evil seamlessly threads its way through secular psychology. Fights against reification and moralism in psychological discourse may implicitly tap into this. Some time ago (Eigen, 1993; Nelson & Eigen, 1984), I tried to show that the devil was very alive psychically and traced workings of demonised aspects of the self. In part, I meant mangled, strangulated aspects of self, personality deformations and warps. But also something more, a will or need to injure, to make another hurt deep inside. A complex, nasty gradient that seemed boundless. As if the more injury one inflicted, the more one needed to inflict. In part, it might be that one was trying to wipe out a sense of injury in oneself, to clean oneself out by injuring another. Once again, arriving at an area of pain.

To blot out the pain of evil: an ancient theme. God wanting to wipe out the human race because of its evils, as if not being able to bear the result of creation. Freud wrote of primal trauma as flooding—an emotional flood or flood of stimulation. He imagined an infant trying to tone down impacts, finding psychical ways to blunt pain. In one scenario, he imagined a baby hallucinating the presence of the breast, replacing the distress of hunger with imaginary satisfaction. Freud lets us wonder how and to what extent and with what consequences we replace painful realities with imaginary, even delusional scenarios.

On the other side, there is a tendency to inflict injury on oneself to escape pain. I once heard James Grotstein share his fantasy of an infant destroying its corpus callosum in order to escape the pain of meaning. Imagine the possibility of destroying aspects of one's own brain in order to escape the pain of experience. Bion (1994) does something parallel by writing about mind destroying itself in face of what it cannot bear. War may have a similar function, like God destroying the universe in order to blot out the pain of evil. In the case of war, pain is used to blot out pain. Massive injury to blot out and/or make visible injury within.

As mentioned before, we do not usually call all the destruction in the universe evil. There are natural disasters with no malignant intention, although when one moves past a point, for example, thinking of terrible deformities or ills befalling a child, an idea of evil begins creeping in. What kind of universe is this in which such things can happen? Chance, the luck of the draw the difference between curse and blessing.

Lautréamont (2004) attempted to depict a character, Maldoror, with purely evil intention, evil mind. Not just evil imagination, evil intention, but evil essence. He did so with great success, stimulating surrealist literature. Lautréamont (Comte de Lautréamont) was a pseudonym for Isidore-Lucien Ducasse, born in Uraguay and died in Paris in 1870 at the age of twenty-four. Although not much is known about him, I picture him mostly alone wandering the streets of Paris, increasingly taken by a fervent vision of absolute evil in a human being. Just as God's mediating vessels broke under the strain of creation (Eigen, 2012a), so did Lautréamont's shell give way mediating a purely evil character. An act of fiction, to be sure, but channelling and expressing a gradient of our nature. I think, too, of a story by Isaac Bashevis Singer (I no longer remember its name) in which an old exorcist frees a haunted mansion of the spirit of Lilith, but is found spread-eagled in the morning snow, unable to survive what he had to bear.

Levinas (1969, 1999) wrote about destructive aspects of the life force, our élan. Our vital life feeling can tend towards violent pursuit of desires, self-interest that could injure others, a tendency on a psychological level that seems built into violent aspects of being. His work is a kind of critique of being and a call for other than being. He writes of a need to be fully responsible for others, beyond our own needs. A kind of variation and amplification of the perennial theme of narcissism–socialism, selfishness–altruism. He also stresses not knowing what may be needed in a given situation and building capacity for creative waiting (Eigen, 2005). Creative waiting while faced with emotional pulls tends to give way to premature simplification, partly a result of not being able to sustain the build-up of psychic forces without precociously discharging them.

Lautréamont's depiction of absolute evil is a radical simplification as a kind of lens for exploration. We may have at stake something like this as part of our complex make-up in tension with other forces or tendencies and capacities. Whatever Lautréamont meant by total or absolute evil, it fired up areas of French literature, a source of inspiration and inflammation. The idea of absolute evil has traction, grabs, does not let go. If we press the lever that switches tracks of meaning, we have Bion (1965; Eigen, 1996, 1998, 2004, 2005, 2010, 2011b) writing of "a force that goes on working after it destroys existence, time and space". A force that feeds on destruction after all else is gone. A current in human life dedicated to destroying.

We know how good it can be to knock down barriers or knock down a tower of blocks we built. The feeling of breaking through constriction as part of a feeling of freedom sometimes pushes us towards new areas of experiencing. Destruction can be part of autonomy and growth. Yet, it is a tendency that can go haywire, feed on itself, a gradient or will or sense of doing away with everything.

I have heard people say, "I feel guilty for creating death." And some say, "I create death to be free. I kill to be free, to clear an area of freedom." Megalomania–impotence extends in both directions.

I created everything that is. I am able to create or be nothing. Nothing–everything feeding a sense of imprisonment–freedom, two states reversing, turning inside out: a freeing nothing, an imprisoning nothing, a freeing everything, an imprisoning everything. I tug against limits, push against barriers, try to break through walls and shells of personality, try to break through nothing and everything.

William Blake associated the devil with energy and called energy eternal delight. Jesus was Creative Imagination, which Satan fed. Kwan Yin, a Chinese Buddha, expresses the opposite tendency of Bion's force that destroys. She can only be compassionate, granting wishes of seekers, asking nothing in return save, perhaps, thank you. A translation of one of her names is, "she who hearkens to the cries of the world".

Mythic depictions of a force that gives and a force that takes away. In a temple I visited in Kyoto, there was what I call a Buddha sandwich with Kwan Yin at the top. The sandwich was filled with demon Buddhas, one on top of the other, layers of the psyche or spirit, and at the top, Kwan Yin (Kammon in Japan). I took it partly to portray many psychic tendencies which could pull each other apart and destroy the whole without a primacy of the Kwan Yin principle, compassion, to modulate, guide, mediate (Eigen, 1995, 1998, 2010).

Lines between madness, creativity, and evil can, at times, seem very thin. Kusama, the Japanese artist, is a benign example of fusion of psychosis and creativity. After a try at life in the outside world in New York, she had to, perhaps preferred to, live in a mental hospital in Japan, which gave her safety to pursue her life's work as an artist (http://youtu.be/rRZR3nsiIeA).

Even today, when I read newspaper reports of someone shooting people in a school or office, often ending by shooting themselves, accounts often meld madness and evil. On the one hand, the killers are seen as individuals burdened by mental health problems, and today legislation is being considered to help those so distressed by mental illness that evil acts might be result. At the same time, a line can be crossed when the emphasis is not on illness but evil: how could someone do such evil things. They *must* be evil.

Psychopathy is no longer a popular word. It has been changed to sociopathy, to emphasise the environmental aspect of the difficulty, an extremely narcissistic form of socialisation with possible environmental wounds. I once heard Henry Elkin (1972) link psychopathy with maternal patterns that aroused excitement to a peak, then turned off, placing the infant in a chronic seesaw of tantalisation. One gets the sensory–emotional high, then plunge, the switch abruptly turns off to nothingness, from heightened stimulation to being dropped off the edge of the universe. The two phases become fused in a single system, an individual high and dead at the same time, caught in an impossible position of too much–too little at once. If this is so, it might account for some cases in which one person needs to elicit arousal in another only to betray it.

Winnicott (1990) tends to associate delinquency with early gratification giving way to deprivation. In this case, criminality is a sign of hope, an attempt to get something for oneself, while enacting the sense of deprivation through the other's loss, turning the tables. There is a Zen story about the village thief being caught and brought to the Zen master for punishment, who suggests hanging the man from a tree with a halter that does not hurt, and bringing him everything he wants. He is to be treated well, royally. Perhaps an idea implicit here is to facilitate an experience of being given to without having to get it by oneself, a kind of redressing wounded dependency. This reflects a sense learnt early in life that if one is to get something one cannot rely on others, but has to get it for oneself any way one can.

Recent brain studies (Intratur et al., 1997; Meffert et al., 2013) seem to find differences in brain patterns for psychopaths, including differences of blood flow for emotional words and mirroring patterns involving empathy. In the latter case, it is not that empathy is totally lacking, but it does not arise spontaneously while witnessing distress in others. It can be elicited with special effort, suggesting capacity to tune into others can be turned on and off. In one scenario, empathic capacity can be used to gauge the victim and sense how to manipulate him or her, while remaining cool to get what one wants: empathy in the service of psychopathy. I suspect this is a tendency that is part of personality more generally, an aspect of survival strategies that can hypertrophy.

A more sinister but, I fear, too common ploy is psychopathic manipulation of psychotic anxieties. For example, creating or playing on delusional annihilation dreads: For example, Iraq has weapons of mass destruction that threaten us or our allies and we better get them before they get us. Do we know why we went to war with Iraq? Power, oil, position in the area? Certainly not about imagined weapons of mass destruction as a real threat. A giant con job playing on mass fears. The phrase "self-interest" was used a lot, but I have begun to wonder if we know what our or anyone's self-interest is. Examples can be easily multiplied, illustrating insensitivity to pain, mutilation, and deaths inflicted by following "self-interest". For more explorations of psychopathic manipulation of psychotic anxieties see my online book, *Age of Psychopathy* (2006b) (www.psychoanalysis-and-therapy.com/human_nature/eigen/pref.html).

When I was in training, I would hear that psychoanalysis could not be effective if the patient and analyst were not committed to truth. Often, Truth with a capital T. Freud felt psychosis was not amenable to psychoanalysis and the dictum that you cannot psychoanalyse a liar puts psychopathy out of bounds, too. Since that time, there has been a veritable explosion of analytic approaches to psychosis with life-saving effectiveness for many (Eigen, 1986). My feeling is that we must develop response capacity capable of working with psychopathy as well. Not only are individual lives at stake, but society's health, too, since financial psychopathy has become a norm. Bion notes that lying is ubiquitous. It has many functions, protective, imaginative, but also destructive. Being destructive can be gratifying. There is pleasure in destruction, even in causing pain or worse, a tendency that can mushroom into danger or play a creative role in a larger whole. When people tell me you cannot psychoanalyse a liar, I joke, "If you can't psychoanalyse a liar, who *can* you psychoanalyse, considering a liar is doing the psychoanalysing." Developing response capacity to work with our psychopathic streak, which for some becomes a dominant, is essential for human evolution (Eigen, 2006b).

* * *

In the public mind there often is a wedding between psychopathy and psychosis, a sense that madness and murder are linked, for example, the phrase, "psychotic killer". In ape groups, depressed or berserk members are usually isolated, groups sensing danger to the group. In human life, different tendencies may fuse, so that category differences can be fluid. The matter is complex and we cannot do justice to it here. On the human plane, psychosis may be feared and ostracised, but may also be seen as a gateway to certain forms of wisdom, madman/madwoman as seer. There are also attempts to see a psychotic individual as ill, needing help rather than godly or demonic.

Here, I would like to share an exploration into aspects of "the psychotic ego" or "demonized aspects of self" (Eigen, 1986, 1993) in one individual, shouting "Kill, kill, kill." He made his way to my office after a four-month hospital stay, treated by insulin shock and thorazine. Electroshock was also used, but doctors quickly realised it was making things worse. The patient, Lewis, said of it, "It wasn't the convulsion that was the worse thing. That was bad enough. The world around me broke into pieces. It was horrible that the world was inhabited by devils everywhere. But to see the devils broken in pieces, shards, like broken glass. And not only the devils, and this is the main point. The world itself, the perceptual space I lived in and took for granted—sky, earth, trees—and much harder to convey, space itself. Space itself convulsed, broke into pieces. Everything was in pieces."

Everything shattered. This was in the 1960s and I could not avoid thinking of the phrase, "disintegration of the ego", a common phrase in the therapy field at that time to describe aspects of psychosis. A picture formed in me that Lewis's shattered ego was fused with the world. But I also took in that the world broken in pieces was more than terrifying. It shattered any sense of perceptual security. Shattered self, shattered world.

It is often said that in psychosis there are ways the world remains intact. A person does not walk into trees. On one level, he sees things as they are, like everyone else. Lewis, too, saw people as they are. He did not bump into people. He kept proper distances, knew where things were, could tell the difference between men and women, recognised people, their names, retained a sense of the other's identity, lay down or sat on the couch, seemed to automatically feel that something was to happen between us. He called me Dr Eigen, and coming four times a week for the first few years provided continuity in his life. He drove to my New York office from Westchester.

Not only were there aspects of continuity in the external world, but inside, too. Freud wrote of an observing ego, a witness, watching even in the midst of psychotic cataclysm (Eigen 1986, Chapter One). Many speak of the mad in the normal and the normal in the mad. And while the observer shattered for a time, pieces of the shatter or something elusive beneath them kept witnessing.

Lewis was hospitalised when he began seeing people as devils. The devil was mainly in facial expressions. A voice commanded him to do as it said or he would be damned forever. Ostensibly, he did not want to be hospitalised but he could not decide about anything any longer. He was partly paralysed. Should he do this, should he do that? He was afraid to follow the voice, afraid not to. A psychiatrist his parents brought him to ordered hospitalisation, which came as a relief to all, although also leaving Lewis defeated, entrapped, helpless. He thought less of himself for lacking the power to follow the voice. He felt he would never think well of himself again.

"I saw evil everywhere, yet powerless to do anything about it. The voice would not tell me what it wanted in a way that enabled me to do it. The gap between order and action was too great. One moment I felt it wanted me to kill, to attack the devils, rid the world of evil. One moment it wanted me to kill strangers on the street, another moment those close to me. It wanted me to throw myself in front of a subway train just to prove my faith. It's not that I stopped seeing people as people. But they were run by devils. A devil was in their facial expression, *was* their facial expression."

On the one hand, Lewis felt impotent to kill anyone, yet mumbled under his breath, "Kill, kill, kill." Sometimes, he was compelled to run down a street yelling at the top of his lungs, "Kill, kill, kill." Damned forever because he did not do what the voice wanted. It was amazing that he was not locked up before his parents brought him to a psychiatrist. It was as if screaming on the street created a space around him, a hollow, as if he were invisible, inaudible.

So, here are some elemental rudiments of evil possibilities, devils and the command to kill, a sense of damnation and weakness for failure of will, which might push some on and over, a dare to be answered.

As time went on, Lewis was able to describe the devils in more detail, how in some they were layered, almost painted on, and in others they seemed to cover the skin from below the surface. Not like tattoos—they were inspirited beings. Frightening spirits materialising before his eyes, feeling like a revelation of the human condition. After some time together, he said that although he condemned himself for his weakness and inability to act, he was not able to get his body to do it. I said, "It sounds like your body is smarter than you are."

The body's fear as a kind of wisdom. Lewis was lucky. Something in his body would not go along with the voice, the death wish. The body wanted to live, afraid of death. "God told me to kill and jump in front of a train but my body wouldn't listen and I blamed myself."

"Sounds like you have God and the devil mixed up," I said. The logjam was beginning to loosen. A hairsbreadth and it could have gone otherwise.

I think of God ordering Abraham to kill Isaac and Freud's depiction of the tension in Michelangelo's Moses wrestling with his fury (Eigen, 2005). Here, art depicts conflicting tensions that beset us, emotional pressures that can drive us mad or towards psychopathy or creativity. I think of the Rabbi Akiva story about the "garden". Four men go into the garden. One goes mad, one kills himself (I might add, or becomes a killer), one becomes a heretic, and Rabbi Akiva comes out glowing. Of course, all those possibilities and more are in us, but so is the Rabbi Akiva aspect.

As part of our multi-faceted work, I asked Lewis, when I felt he could begin to stand it, to look at the devils, stare at them, study them. Perhaps pick one out or see which he gravitates to, which pulls him. Even stare at it until he goes blank, something he could not do for some time, because the fear was too great. But the work of transformation had begun.

"As I stare I see my father's face embedded in the devil face. My angry father, yelling in outbursts you scarcely knew when, I suppose when frustration overpowered him, but it was a blast that shocked, petrified. That's something else I see, petrification, the devil petrifying a face. Freezing the face. I hate it that my face feels frozen. I wish I had a fluid, full expression instead of looking petrified. My face underwent a process of petrification I remain trapped in.

"I'm looking straight at, in, through the devil and see my father and now my face. My father's is part of the devil face, mine is not. Mine is a petrified face, stone. Maybe that's part of what gets me through things, how I may be getting through this, iron, stone, sticking it out. Something in me like a locomotive that won't stop. Not even for devils.

"I caught myself in a lie. I *did* stop. My heart stopped beating. But now I'm going again, still going. Something won't give up. The devil is my father's face, my father is the devil's face. But I see my own ego in the face as well, a deformed ego, rotten, poisoned, tight like a fist, crippled. My own ego is the devil too. But it is not all me. I also live somewhere else. I can look at my sick self, a sickness I always felt that became the devil. I am still scared but I am looking. I am seeing."

I ask Lewis when he sees devils, does he ever see anything else?

"In the hospital I saw some people as more devil than others. I would look at one and say, 'He's a devil,' and I might find something less or non-devil in someone else.

"In the hospital I met a girl and we became friends and had an affair and I never saw her as a devil. I saw her pain, her love, her need, her strength. It was easy for us to be with each other, a comfort, a relief. So now, after all this time, I can say the devil was not all there was. There was goodness too, but it failed to placate the devil.

"Sometimes I fear a flicker of devil in you but I have never seen you as a devil, or just devil. It took me a while to catch on to this—but when we met after the hospital the devil was missing in your face, although there were flickers. And now that I think on it, I noticed this was so in the hospital too, but was not sure what to make of it. I was puzzled. Could I be wrong? Was I seeing wrong, thinking wrong? I did not know what was real. The devil felt really real.

"Now when I look at my father devil I see a pained face. What a wounded life! And what a locomotive puffing through it! Going on, on. Iron. A pained face inside the devil. My ego devil, too, wracked with pain. My father drank a lot when I was growing up but I never quite understood that it was to blunt the pain.

"I get the strangest thought. That I see devils not just to show the pain but to blunt it."

Where is the evil? Evil averted? The evil of life that twists one out of shape, the pain that deforms? And some are lucky to live on without, finally, killing others or themselves. Some reach points of compassion.

* * *

Bion's writings are filled with examples of states that play an important role in psychotic dynamics. He emphasises an abrupt change from good or neutral to bad. One is going along all right enough, then the rug is pulled out from under. Here are some examples.

> "Well then, if you want to know," he said, becoming confidential, "last night I had a most enjoyable evening. People smoking, intelligent, friendly atmosphere, and then . . .," becoming indignant in a noisy voice, "the waitress brought me only half a cup of coffee, and that ab-so-lutely finished it." Dropping his voice, "I couldn't do a thing after that. Not a thing." Almost whispering, "That finished it." (*Cogitations*, 1994, p. 79)

The patient says, 'Suddenly, just as I finished lunch he threw a mug of beer in my face without any warning. I kept my head and showed no resentment at all remembering what you had said about psychoanalysis. So it passed off without anyone noticing.' (*Attention and Interpretation*, 1970, p. 3)

X said . . . well, what? He used words in such a way that they seemed to indicate that his mother or relatives had cut off supplies; that he could sell out $500 of shares and go to the cottage, in which case there would only be $50 and that just could not buy food. "That's all there is to it." (*Cogitations*, p. 29)

All of the three examples above, as well as others, delineate a rapid, extreme change and in two a helplessly totalistic reaction. Half a cup, mug in the face, cut off supplies: "I couldn't do a thing after that. Not a thing . . . That finished it." "That's all there is to it."

We are, in part, speaking about pain, trauma, a sharp cut, neglect, intrusion without capacity to recover well. The individuals he writes of seem to have a very sensitive underbelly and at the same time a rigid exoskeleton they are trapped in. A kind of hell. Violence of a kind that renders one impotent, encased in injury in the face of which one feels almost resourceless. Here, Bion describes work with psychotic dynamics with traumatic components, adumbratively mirrored in daily events. One might say that he depicts elements of post-trauma shock bound by mixtures of lability–rigidity. Shock long since lost in silence, but forceful in everyday life.

It is not hard to imagine explosive outbursts in some individuals under impinging pressures without resources to modulate them. Part of explosive reactiveness sometimes involves using violence to blot out violence and right perceived wrongs (Eigen, 2002). Bion, too, depicts traumatic explosiveness (1970; Eigen, 1998) oscillating and fusing with massive emotional shutdown. Lines between unbearable pain, emotional violence, and what we would call evil acts can be terribly thin.

In an autobiographical work (1982, pp. 21–22), Bion recounts his delight as a boy having an air gun, which snapped on his thumb while loading it, pleasure turning into bloody screams. "Whoever is that screaming? Screaming. Screaming. Screaming. Oh God my throbbing hand! . . . blood everywhere." His mother tries to comfort him, dress the wound; father speaks of bravery. "There! It doesn't hurt much does it?" "But it throbs; bang, bang, bang it goes. Why does my heart beat like that in my thumb?" His mother tries to soothe, quiet him, "Shsh, it's only a dream, go to sleep, my darling." He concludes, "The scar on my thumb is clear now, seventy years later. I don't suppose it made much scar on my mind because I do not remember a time when I wasn't a sissy."

Here, like his patients, the pattern is adumbrated. Pain, pain, pain, scream, scream, scream, throb, bang, bang, bang and the natural parental effort to quiet and soothe the pain away. A pain that entered the stream of being as lasting emotional pain one fears or is unable to tolerate contact with, but which has an impact on a life. It is, Bion feels, a problem of the human condition. What do we do with emotional pain? To what extent can we sustain, modulate, work with it and how? Bion feels our capacity to work with emotional life is embryonic, an evolutionary challenge. Emotional pressures easily become too much for us. We turn them down as we can, work with them as we can. Some rare individuals, Shakespeare for one, may transmute them into art—for example, his depictions of madness, murder, unbearable states that mirror bits of psychic agony that play a role in who we are and what we do.

Why one person becomes an artist of pain and another a heinous murderer is often beyond knowing. We make guesses. I have heard that Wittgenstein and Hitler were in the same class in school. One was left back, the other skipped. One became a philosopher, the other a mass murderer. Wittgenstein could not have had an emotionally easy background. Three of his brothers killed themselves; another was autistic. But he had a background of wealth and culture that Hitler lacked. I cannot help finding it hard to imagine he would become a mass killer if he had Hitler's background. And what of Hitler's background, his lack of support and failure as an artist, homeless for a time, smouldering resentment and growing nationalism—how could such horrifying evil grow out of pain?

We are amazing in our plasticity and persistence, beings who can make some kind of go of it in almost any conditions. Haunted by death and evil. The pain of life has caused various religions to see this life as evil. Some locate the cause in material, others in spiritual, dimensions. The books of Moses end with an open-ended choice to be made between good and evil, the outcome in doubt. Freud rephrases the dilemma, wondering whether or not the life drive will prevail over the death drive. What will human beings do? Bion reworks this evolutionary challenge in terms of our relation to our emotional life. Will we find better ways to partner our experiential capacity, learn from experience, support growth of experience, or will lack of capacity provoke attempts to attack and destroy emotional life that can be so painful? Many of us may want to wish evil and death away and some become destructive in face of destruction, as if, like God in Genesis, trying to blot out facts that are resistant to change. Rabbis tell us part of the reason Cain killed Abel was that he did not wait long enough to let a painful experience become absorbed, he reacted too quickly to a slight he could not bear, potential growth short-circuited. He could not let experience build. I suspect human beings have made intermittent attempts to build more of an emotional digestive system over the past several thousand years, an attempt that has a long way to go. So much of our lives are affected by emotional indigestion and its consequences.

The great work of Shakespeare often melds psychopathy, madness, evil, and desperation in face of oneself. At one point, having tasted the consequences of his nature, or, as Freud might say, his character collapsing on itself, Shakespeare has Macbeth say to the physician, "Canst thou not minister to a mind diseased?"

Bion's (1977) response to this line was: "Not now. But come back in two hundred years and we'll see what we can do."

CHAPTER SIX

Tiger stripes and student voices

I began teaching W. R. Bion in the 1970s and D. W. Winnicott in the 1960s. I met Winnicott in 1968 and Bion in 1977. Both were important not only to my psychoanalytic learning, but to my personal growth. Their example enhanced permission to be me.

In the one week I saw Bion in New York, he told me to stop analysis and get married. He said, "Marriage isn't what you think. It's two people telling truth to each other, helping to mitigate the severity to yourself." I was forty-one, in and out of relationships. His remark initiated a series of events that in three years led to my becoming a married father. Something in his mien and manner reached me, enabling what I had wanted to do for decades.

How did this happen? Other parts of the time we spent together also are bearing fruit, some only now as a senior citizen. Out of the blue, he asked me about the Kabbalah, then after brief discussion paused and remarked, "I use the Kabbalah as a framework for psychoanalysis." I met Bion less than two years before he died. Now I am almost his age when we met and have recently published books exploring links between Bion and Kabbalah (Eigen, 2012a, 2014a,b).

I started teaching Bion before we met. I knew the group book and papers on psychotic thinking and used them in my courses. What exerted a greater pull was the series of amazing works that came out in the 1960s, which overlapped with his own sixties and early seventies, particularly, *Learning from Experience*, *Elements of Psychoanalysis*, *Transformations*, and, for me, a climactic, life-changing work, *Attention and Interpretation*. I needed to read these works closely and as an aid began teaching *Learning from Experience*, the first of this series. I taught in order to learn. We did a little at a time, relishing trails, phrases, or words, or paragraphs opened. A sense of psychic reality opened before our eyes. Trails taking us through psychotic turns of mind, bursting or trickling off into mystic moments.

Gradually, I moved from K-Bion to F-Bion, not that the two are unrelated. Earlier in my teaching, there was more emphasis on K and –K, linking and attacks on linking, knowing (K) and attacks on knowing. One might say love of *vs.* hatred of knowing. Knowing reality, psychic reality, emotional reality. A nexus linked with mind–mindlessness. Having and using one's mind, so to speak, *vs.* ridding oneself of this disturbing vehicle, through which one often sees and hears and learns things one would rather not know, intolerable things, intolerable no-things (Eigen, 1996).

In my first book (1986), I included a chapter called "Mindlessness", in which I discussed the difficulties Bion raised with regard to being a mindful creature, difficulties in tolerating tensions that are part of mental life. It touched one of his hallmark concerns, evacuation of mental processes to avoid psychic pain. To avoid psychic pain, one may attempt to destroy capacities that experience it, including the possibility of destroying one's own mind in order to avoid contact with intolerable perceptions, intolerable emotional realities. Instead of facing and modulating—destruction. Or, as fits reality, both.

Bion wrote of most dreams being semi-aborted, since only so much build-up of emotion is tolerable. In *Cogitations* (1994) he suggests that psychic intensity can damage psychic functioning. The psyche cannot take itself, or can only take so much of itself. There are moments when use of psychic capacity to digest damaging processes can suffer damage. In such an instance, we are in the predicament of becoming damaged by our attempts to process damage. For example, dream work can be damaged by the dreaming process, creating a situation in which damaged dream work tries to express and digest damaging emotions. Throughout his work, Bion often portrays situations with no solution, no way out—situations one must sit with, tolerate, grow through (Eigen, 2009, 2010, 2011a,b, 2012a).

Once I started to teach *Attention and Interpretation* (1970), I could not stop. I taught it for many years and one of my students is now teaching it. I include a little "pony" to parts of "Chapter Two: The medical model", in *The Psychoanalytic Mystic* (1998). F in O is central to *Attention and Interpretation*, F in O and T in O (I made a little chant of these two notations in *Kabbalah and Psychoanalysis*, 2012a). Faith in O, the latter a notation for unknowable, emotional reality and T in O, unknown transformations in O, which although unknown, may have an impact on us.

Bion calls Faith the psychoanalytic attitude, a state of being without memory, expectation, understanding, or desire, radically open. An ideal, of course, but a path, a practice. He feels it necessary for repair and growth of intuition. Since one of his special interests is psychotic experiencing and functioning, the O of moment may be "known" or intuited via catastrophic impacts. O as ultimate emotional reality is sometimes characterised as a catastrophic Origin, in which case a sense of catastrophe links personality together, cements or binds personality. A sense of disintegration organises personality.

What has Bion done in bringing faith and catastrophe together? For one thing, he is nakedly honest. Clearly, not all life is catastrophic. There is much joy, pleasure, beauty, bliss, goodness. Yet, catastrophe is a thread that runs through it, sometimes more, sometimes less. Psychoanalysis notes that the very push and pressure of being an emotional being has catastrophic aspects and consequences. We are a very destructive as well as creative group and I suspect we are in infancy in learning what to do with our destructiveness, if such learning is possible for humankind. Whether or not we succeed in learning what to do with destructiveness, we are giving it a try.

Faith in the face of catastrophic O. An extraordinary nucleus in the depths of our feeling life. An emotional nucleus that is part of what I call a basic rhythm: breaking, shattering, going under, dying, and coming through (Eigen, 2004). An emotional nucleus and clinical attitude that Bion and Winnicott share.

Some scholars see the Kabbalah as a response to catastrophe. It touches dimensions in which faith, mystical experience, and catastrophe are linked. The link between faith and catastrophe is an emotional conjunction, or nucleus, that takes many forms in psycho-spiritual life.

One of the most striking phrases that give expression to this moment is Job's "Yay, though You slay me yet will I trust You." Another is Jesus, "Father, why have you forsaken me?" In the face of death, faith. In the face of loss of faith, faith. For Bion, faith is a vehicle that radically opens experiencing and plays a role in building tolerance for experience. At the same time, he does not minimise what we are up against, the full force of destructiveness. He has one of the strongest formulations of the destructive force I ever read. He writes of a destructive force that goes on destroying after it destroys personality, time, existence (Bion, 1965, p. 101). He puts a tracer on what seems like pure destructive capacity. This is what faith faces, must face. It is germane to the fervour and possibility of existence, a tension, struggle, sense that has an impact on the flavour of our lives.

At some point, I felt I could go on teaching *Attention and Interpretation* forever, but also needed to do something else. I wanted to teach *A Memoir of the Future* (1991) and felt reading *Cogitations* would be good preparation. I have been teaching *Cogitations* for over fifteen years with over a hundred pages to go.

When I pick a section for an Institute class, there are often students who feel lost without historical overview or birds-eye summary of Bion's thought. I recommend readings for that. But there also are students who want to dive in, feel liberated by focusing on a bit of terrain and letting it build. Over the course of a semester, I do try to give a bit of overview, usually growing out of problems inherent in the reading. In the end, some leave frustrated. But it is worth teaching this way for those who find it nourishing, who feel doors opening.

This was something I found my way to early in my teaching life, not just with Bion, but years before in universities and training programmes. I could only teach what I loved and was happy if lights went on for one or two students. The class gave them something needed, something they might not have known existed. I taught the way I wanted to be taught, out of the depths of my being with a living sense of psychic reality. In time, I tried to write that way, too, and sometimes was lucky. I gravitated to Bion and Winnicott because they did that for me, opened my windows, my living being.

Processes Bion touches feel real to me and, to the extent I can, I try to mediate them, open them. I go for the jugular in each class, plunge in, take off. Teaching my private seminar has advantages. For one thing, it is self-selective. Those who find it meaningful to work this way stay. Those for whom it is senseless or intolerable leave. My private seminar has been ongoing for nearly forty years and is well attended. I feel there is a hunger for intense work, bites of psychic apples that grow as you chew. I guess I made a choice long ago. I am not for everyone, and neither is Bion. But for some who tune in, what happens opens reality.

When I teach Bion, Bion teaches me. Or perhaps something happens that is not quite either of us, x, "it". I learn as I teach. Things come out I had no idea about moments before. Much of my writing on Bion grew out of living moments in class. I often say about Rilke that he creates realities as he writes. His words create existence. Bion is terrific for this. Immerse yourself in a phrase, a section, a paragraph and speak, and reality opens, you open, some class members open. We are taken to places we did not expect and might not have reached ourselves. Not every writer has this capacity. If you think of the deadening quality of so many psychoanalytic publications, you appreciate all the more the opening of living reality by some.

There are pithy sentences throughout Bion's work. One cannot read any of his works without at least one sentence that strikes an alarm, touches a nerve, makes you wince, gives permission to think and feel. His work can intrigue, and evoke wonder. Just as you think things could not be worse, he takes you further into a mangled aspect of psyche, desolation, demolition. You want to say, things cannot be this bad, then realise that in the background of your being you are shaking.

Rilke emphasises trembling. Near the beginning of the Bible, God's "hovering" can be translated as "trembling". Bion taps psychic tremors in the background. A film I recently saw, *Beasts of the Southern Wild*, touches aspects of nameless dread in our psychic substratum. From time to time, ancient beasts romped through scenes of current life, reminders of imminent annihilation. At one point, a girl faced them—the horrors of our minds, the horrors of existence—and, for a moment, they backed off.

At another point in the film, the girl's father tells her that his blood is eating itself, a way of letting her know he is dying. The point of dread changes location. The Bible says the soul is in the blood. And here the soul eats itself.

"Yay, though You slay me . . ."

I will give some Bion quotes I like. I could pick others. You could and should pick others. You could give classes on any of them. Like the beasts in the film, they are parts of threads that appear throughout Bion's work. Franz Kafka said his life was an incomplete moment. Perhaps all moments are incomplete. I believe in moments. As Keats writes, "A thing of beauty is a joy forever". Or William Blake, "All states are eternal". There is something deeply beautiful about Bion's work, something beautiful about psychoanalysis, even if often a dark beauty, a dark radiance. Perhaps precisely because he does not flinch, his work is uplifting. When we spoke, Bion brought up *Zohar*, a principal book of Kabbalah, meaning splendour or radiance. It is no accident that the book of radiance encompasses catastrophic realities.

"The fundamental reality is 'infinity', the unknown, the situation for which there is no language – not even one borrowed by the artist or the religious – which gets anywhere near to describing it" (*Cogitations*, p. 372).

As mentioned earlier, Bion uses "O" as a notation for "the fundamental reality". In Judaism, YHVH connotes a fundamental reality for which there is no language, concept, or image. We keep reaching for what cannot be thought or imaged or said, but a term such as God or YHVH already seems so limiting. A formation already in process of becoming a belief system, rather the non-formable, open faith linked to what cannot be known.

Bion calls the latter "infinity", reminiscent of Kabbalah's *Ein Sof*, infinity, no bounds, an attempt to get beyond names like "God". We keep trying to find ways to touch, express, evoke the untouchable. "Infinity" also seems limiting. What is the wordless sense poets seek to evoke with words, or the imageless "feel" artists seek to evoke with image, or that Buddhists express with "emptiness". Perhaps these are ways we try to give expression to boundless, limitless moments, infinity moments, when walls fade. Empty or cup running over—free from being hemmed in by oneself or personality, even an instant, just so, more—soul as water fall, blossom, rainbow, no, that does not get it either. *Ein Sof* moments—no *Ein Sof*. Categories get in the way, fade away. Saint Paul comes a little closer, speaking about moments of grace, not knowing if he has a body, mind, spirit . . . just grace.

Here is another Bion quote: "Psycho-analysis itself is just a stripe on the coat of the tiger. Ultimately it may meet the Tiger – The Thing Itself – O" (*A Memoir of the Future*, 2001, I: 112)

Not just a hand on the elephant, but part of the elephant itself, part of the tiger. We will meet what we are part of, the thing itself, the Real, O. We are reality writing, thinking, speaking, sensing, living. We are it. The separation is part of it. The union is part of it. To meet it itself? Does Bion, whose work is so tied to a sense of evolving, reach for the absolute? We have a hunger for reality. How odd to be part of reality yet hunger for it. We fight to get past lies, seduction, exploitation, feeling them less true, although they are reality, too. We do not feel wholly real. We divide experience into illusion and reality, create sides, yet the terms of our divisions often reverse and turn the latter upside down. Perhaps what we mean when we say we need to get past lies is we need to get past ourselves, that we feel ourselves an impediment, a weight that lifts in moments of grace.

We are and are not wholly "it". One of my favourite quotes is Eddington's "Something unknown is doing we don't know what" (1928, p. 291). We are that unknown which Bion says we can somewhat intuit. There is discordance between living and knowing. We can be at-one with ourselves but not be able to know what that means. At-onement a sense faith touches, mystery part of it.

We are paradoxical beings touched by faith, critical of everything. Critical faith, complex faith. Sincere beings critical of our own nature, perhaps critical of nature itself. Faith that transcends ourselves, includes, yet seeks to go beyond, nature, shed limits. Perhaps one reason numbers zero and one are so appealing, as are imaginary numbers and infinity. A faith bigger than everything. Deeper than anything. Sometimes, I call God the Deepest of All. I think of phrases from the psalms such as "out of the depths I call to you", depth to depth.

> These poets and artists have their methods of recording their awareness of some sort of influence, stimuli that come from without, the unknown that is so terrifying and stimulates such powerful feelings that they cannot be described in ordinary terms . . . We need to invent some form of articulate speech that could approximate to describing these realities, the phenomena that I cannot possibly describe. (*Cogitations*, p. 369)

Terrifying unknown. Freud spoke of flooding as a primal trauma. Flooded by intensity, emotion, stimulation, nothingness. What our nature produces can be too much for it, ahead of its capacity to process and digest it. Traumatised by incapacity to tolerate, work with, digest what happens to us and within us. Traumatised by our own emotional reality.

Bion reaches for dimensions in which emotional reality is unrepresentable, indescribable. Yet, we keep needing to describe, represent, express, find, reveal, touch. We ache to expose what is hidden, including terrifying presentiments in the background of our beings. We need to hide; we need to show. Psychoanalysis sets a task: if we do not find ways of meeting fears that haunt and beset us, we are in danger. We are in danger anyway, tossed (as Taoist sages say, like rag dolls) by waves of emotional intensities with little capacity to sustain them. Paradoxical beings challenged to develop capacities to work with a baffling nature. We have "successful" moments but it cannot be said that we know what we are doing. When Jesus said, forgive them, they don't know what they are doing, he saw our plight. Change they to we: *we* don't know what we are doing. Perhaps we are asked, or ask ourselves, to do what we cannot do. If that is so, it is a situation worth acknowledging and letting in.

If we keep the great unknown in the foreground, perhaps we can learn more about what we *can* do with less belligerence.

> Many mystics have been able to describe a situation in which it is believed there really is a power, a force that cannot be measured or weighted or assessed by the mere human beings with the mere human mind. This seems to me to be a profound assumption which has hitherto been almost completely ignored, and yet people talk about 'omnipotence' as if they knew what it meant and as if it had a simple connotation. Martin Buber [1970] came much closer to recognizing the realities of the situation when human speech is resorted to . . . When one talks about 'I–You', the significant thing is not the two objects related, but the *relationship* – that is, an open-ended reality in which there is no termination (in the sense that this is understood by ordinary human beings). The language of ordinary human beings is only appropriate to the rational, can describe only the rational, can only make statements in terms of rationality. (*Cogitations*, p. 371)

What is this x, this "power", "force", "relationship" without end? The term "what" does not apply, yet it leads us to a felt sense of "the what" without adequate mode of expression, a sensed "what", state, or "something–nothing" paradoxically alluded to by mystics. Open-ended, unending, measureless reality. I think of Emerson's term

"Power", suggesting nameless, creative force that lifts life, pervades life.

Bion points out that this "force", or "relationship", or "power" (inadequate words) could be, in our terms, positive or negative and all combinations. He gives as an example, the Death Pit of Ur, in which members of family and court are interred with the ruling authority, suggesting a religious force of immense power whether invested in God or state or other sources of numinous belief and customs. We are gripped by something and create images, sounds, words, and gestures that give quasi-expression to what grips us, semi-organised forms for a more or less formless sense. Do we have capacity to oscillate between, and work with, the impact of various states of being? Can such a linking capacity develop? What might it look like? Bion suggests the psychoanalyst functions as a bridge between states of mind while awake and asleep, mediating intercourse between psychic dimensions.

> All my life I have been imprisoned, frustrated, dogged by commonsense, reason, memories, desires and – greatest bug-bear of all – understanding and being understood. This is my attempt to express my rebellion, to say 'Good-bye' to all that. It is my wish, I now realized doomed to failure, to write a book unspoiled by any tincture of common-sense, reason, etc. (see above). So although I would write, 'Abandon Hope all ye who expect to find any facts – scientific, aesthetic, religious – in this book', I cannot claim to have succeeded. All these will, I fear, be seen to have left their traces, vestiges, ghosts hidden within these words, even sanity, like 'cheerfulness', will creep in. However successful my attempt, there would always be the risk that the book 'became' acceptable, respectable, honoured, and unread. "Why write then?" you may ask. To prevent someone who knows from filling the empty space – but I fear I am being 'reasonable', that great Ape. Wishing you all a Happy Lunacy and a Relativistic Fission ... (*A Memoir of the Future*, "Epilogue")

One feels limited by one's nature. Bion tries to write from a place without limits and paradoxically explores walls of his nature. He uses intuition to transmit contact with reality. He confesses failure. We are what we are. We try to go further, as if we are driven by unknown possibility, unknown creation. Kabbalah/Chassidus (Schneerson, 1998) suggests the soul is created anew each day. The soul and world is created *ex nihilo* every moment. Bion wishes for this kind of freedom and communicates tastes of moments, possibilities, but we are who we are. We hit our head against our barriers, explore the latter, with an eye beyond.

As the *Kabbalah*, Bion's palette taps many levels of psyche that he can reach, that reach him. Nothing human is foreign. Or, rather, it is all foreign, strange, beckoning, this challenging earth-life, infinities of hells through heavens, and all the shades of green between.

* * *

For much of the remainder of this chapter, I would like to include some of my students, past and present. I asked if anyone would like to write about her or his experience of learning/teaching Bion. Let's dip into some responses.

Student 1. A student who joined my Bion seminar less than three months ago. An experienced analyst with little exposure to Bion. Here is what she wrote.

> "Concerning Bion and the tremendous difficulty I was having understanding him: I found it immensely useful not just to re-read your chapter, "Infinite Surfaces, Catastrophe, Faith" in *The Psychoanalytic Mystic* but also to take notes on it. After I did that, and spent some time trying to explain Bion via Eigen to my husband (who works on Wall Street but can't wait until he retires so he can take philosophy classes again), I had what was actually a quite jarring experience. The next time I opened Bion's *Cogitations*—which was two days later—I read a paragraph that I've read at least five times previously with very little understanding, only this time, I understood so much more that I was really taken aback. I recalled your having said—or written—that understanding Bion is sometimes like gaining vision in a dark cave, when your eyes slowly adjust and gradually, forms come into focus. I've had that experience in the last several weeks but my experience the other day was different. It was much more sudden, like someone unexpectedly raised a window shade on a sunny day. It was so jarring that it was a little weird."

Here is a note the same person wrote on sound and faith and its vicissitudes. In class we were speaking of wordless music, Bion's "doodling in sound", Chassidic "ninguns" (humming/chanting without words, arousing the spirit, traversing a variety of states), Rabbi Nachman's dancing so still he did not seem to move, opening new dimensions of stillness (Eigen, 2012a). She applied some of this to reading a text like Bion's.

"I know this to be true—that I, too, who cannot carry a tune, who can never remember a song or melody, find myself humming. If I take the writings as metaphor for something about the soul expressing/growing/putting something of one's internal world outside oneself, no matter how tentatively and quietly (though, at times, not quietly at all—Bion's screaming explosiveness), I definitely get that.

"I'm reading the chapter you suggested in *The Psychoanalytic Mystic* ["Infinite Surfaces, Explosiveness, Faith"] and want to let you know I've found it incredibly helpful and grounding. I feel that I may be beginning to understand why Bion wrote in his often confusing style. My window into it at this point is that it has to do with him wanting the reader to experience the thing about which she is reading. Point of impact, stripping away intellectualized understanding, staying with experience.

"About faith: I'm beginning to think of it like the air we breathe or the ground we walk on. We tend not to notice it until it's not there. And it's really quite difficult to bring it into focus and hold it in focus—like meditating on one's breathing is difficult. Is Bion saying without faith your aliveness, your emotions become more destructive, that destructive attacks on linking begin to pervade to the point that one's own being is destroyed?

"I have a patient I've seen for fifteen years who this chapter helped me understand. So much of my challenge has been how to help him re-grow a world and psyche in which linking processes can evolve and in which life is possible. (*Attention and Interpretation*, p. 70.) For one thing, this man, who I first saw when he was twenty-one years old, would come in and be unable to talk. "Imprisoned in immobility"— overwhelmed alternatively by the infinite surfaces and then done in by explosiveness. For a 'good girl' like me who was, at that time, on internship and trying to play by the rules, e.g., let the patient speak first, this man blew that all out of the water! At six, he was unable to clean his room, sitting in front of blocks and the box they went in, unable to lift his arm and make it put the blocks in the box. At forty, he sat in his car for five hours at a time, outside his work, unable to go in, unable to leave, unable to phone me or a friend, immobilized. And then he told me of a memory from four, of screaming hysterically, unable to believe that his parents were not coming, that he could not make them come to him. Now he needs to know constantly whether he effects [*sic*] me, does he have an impact on me, what is it, how can he be sure. But most of our work has been without words, outside of words. Psychoanalysis as expanding capacity for experiencing—I like that. Expanding capacity for experiencing variety and intensity. Not as explaining, boxing in, closing down. My analyst and I laughed when we realized that after twenty-one years of work together, my favorite thing that she said was "and then what?"

Student 2: Someone who took a five-class Bion seminar with me through a local institute wrote,

"The class required a change of gears. I initially found the readings and discussion frustratingly non-focussed [sic]. Over time I became aware that this frustration arose in significant degree in response to my reflexive resistance to the "exploded container". I made the connection to my own work with suicidal psychotic patients. It was critically important that I felt comfortable enough to discuss this experience openly in the class. Generally, I have learned not to discuss such things too openly.

"I think that the concept of 'O' and 'F' have been intuitively part of my identity as a clinician since—well, since long before I became a clinician—but that these aspects of myself were something that I was trained to regard as unprofessional or even worse, mystical—training that I have come over the years to increasingly regard as erroneous. Bion offers something more than rebellion—a sense of how to integrate psychoanalysis with the deeper level of human experience."

Student 3: A psychoanalyst, teacher, writer and musician in my private seminar for sixteen years.

"I have been studying Bion in Mike's seminars for sixteen years and never cease to experience a sense of wonder, reverence and awe. I find myself moving into a meditative state and have left the seminar feeling as if I have been immersed in a state of prayer. There is a truth beyond words which gets evoked for me in witnessing and participating in these seminars. We enter deeply into Bion's work, responding to rays of meaning easily overlooked when one reads the text on one's own.

"When I started the seminar we read *Transformations* and eventually moved into *Cogitations*. We stay close to the text, reading a phrase, perhaps an entire sentence, opening Bion's words with clinical and personal associations. Week after week, we may return to the same passage, musically repeating a word, a phrase, cross-referencing what we are reading with other texts. The experience is rich, dynamic and moving. The seminar offers an incredibly nourishing experience for those who want to journey into the infinity of emotional reality Bion's work provides.

"One of the central issues Bion addresses is the primacy of emotional experience and how emotional experience itself is a problem insofar [sic] we have not developed equipment to metabolize, digest, and process our emotional life. Over and over we come back to the challenge each of us is faced with when demands made on us by our emotional life seem more than we can deal with. Echoing the work of Bion, Mike notes ways in which overwhelming emotional experience can deform our psyches or stimulate evolution of equipment needed to partner with the latter. While acknowledging Bion's thoughts on the ubiquity of lying and ways cognition can close as well as open emotional experience, Mike speaks of Bion's notion of faith in face of catastrophe. Even with our fundamental insufficiency in face of emotional life, "unknown intimacies" emerge through contacting unknown–unknowing regions of experience.

"Mike speaks of psychoanalysis as an evolutionary adventure. We are mixed beings "aching to evolve" at the same time mind destroys itself in order not to experience the pain of life on personal, social and political levels. Participating in this seminar has been a transformative and humbling adventure, stimulating my own evolution personally and professionally."

Student 4. A student using my private seminar as partial fulfilment of an institute independent studies course. One thing she likes is jotting down quotes, bits that have moved her.

Bion: ". . . then between the lot of us we can find some kind of response."

She: "We do this in the class, I love how it happens, how you provide the environment for it to happen."

Bion: ". . . when you see your patient tomorrow, will you be able to detect, in the material which is available to you, signs that there is a ghost of a puppet? If you can, you may still be able to breathe some life into that tiny survival."

She: "Applicable at the same time to oneself.

"I like finding how a single line or word or phrase is so rich for meditating on. I think this is what I appreciate most about these three months. The breadth of my familiarity with Bion is much wider, so the close reading is even richer. Gaining access to my own experienced experience.

"Some of what drew me when I began: studying frustration, studying destructiveness, studying omniscience, especially as I need to understand them in relation to my work with patients. I've only scratched the surface. Conscious effort to understand has yielded less than I thought it would.

"Regarding clinical application of Bion's ideas, I have gotten more than I thought I would, but not in the form I expected. It's from Bion's own interactions with people and the way he talks about working with patients. Especially in *The Italian Seminars*, where he keeps bringing it back to "the patient you are going to see tomorrow in your consulting room.

"I love how he busts up all kinds of assumptions (eg, that there are two personalities in the room)—constant dissolving of omniscient positions.

"And at the same time he cares so much about the analyst taking responsibility for the treatment. 'Our problem is to be sensitive to the sufferings of people who come to us for assistance, but not be so affected by them as to interfere with our thinking clearly about the work in hand ... If a patient tries to throw you out of your window, it may be difficult to appreciate that he comes to you because he wants help ...'

"And then: 'This same force which may be manifesting itself in a physical struggle with you, is what he has to live with.' Suddenly I feel deeply for this patient. 'So he may be afraid that you will not be able to resist him physically and is terrified that he himself may not be able to resist or deal with that terrifying force.' Destructiveness in action.

"Back to responsibility: '... But in the position in which we find ourselves – a position which, it could be said, is inherited – we ARE the authority, we ARE the parents ...'

"And then: '... and there is no one else to go to excepting ourselves.'

"What I have absorbed, from hanging out with you and Bion and everyone in the seminar, is hard to describe but I feel it evident in my work. Something having to do with experiencing more, breathing experience rather than managing it. This is what I value most."

Student 5: Poet, author, leader of seminars on spirituality.

"A liberating experience: the dark self gains legitimacy and validation. Faith is stressed as a disposition that supports life, not without fear, but with persistence. Bion's and Eigen's confessional tone prompts a sense of openings to unexpected realities. Sticking with the insoluble becomes grounds for new possibilities. A sense of mystery is welcome. How refreshing to embrace the unknown, while allowing the unconscious and preconscious to unravel, and slowly see the light of day."

Student 6: Psychotherapist who was in my seminar ten years ago for two years and comes to my public events.

She writes about Bion's war experiences, the mark it left, and passages that link sessions to danger, emotional dangers. How does one maintain "sanity" and a "clear head" in the midst of fears and mad realities? She follows lines of destructiveness in our time and moments of possibility. She refers to Bion's autobiographical works and brings up his wife's death in giving birth to their daughter.

"You point out that in his autobiography Bion portrays his immobility when, as a baby, she [his daughter] tried to crawl across the yard to reach him, that he describes how he 'sat in affectless paralysis as she struggled' until the housekeeper, unable to bear anymore, picked her up and hugged her.

"I hadn't read Bion's autobiography until just recently, but from hearing you talk about this incident, I had already been startled that he was willing to share such agony about something that could have made him look bad. I realized that I had already been feeling something for him through your teaching—a deep respect and also something like empathy, not just for him, for everyone including myself. It was a disorienting experience. It made me feel there was a great humility about him, something I feel for you as well. Humility and compassion.

"As many students of Bion have said, Bion is not easy. I believe that one way you helped learning about him is by spending a year or so on one sentence. That has become an affectionate joke and it's hard to believe unless one has been there—moving away from the sentence and back again and again starting over and over from the same/different place, trusting your ability seamlessly to introduce literature, poetry, philosophy, mathematics, physics, philosophy, your own clinical experience, making it possible to drift almost unconsciously a little deeper without having to make immediate sense of it. It's been immensely helpful to me in feeling my own catastrophes, my faith and lack of faith, being damaged, damaging others, being loved, loving others, feeling broken, paralyzed, and recovering over and over, opening up to bear a little more of what I'm experiencing of what makes me "me", enjoying both the hard work and moments of grace.

"And sometimes it feels like too much to me. Like I've just found "the truth", a place to rest for awhile and, before I know it, it feels like you're destroying my secure place. It's a little like Leonard Cohen's line "There Is a Crack in Everything, That's How the Light Gets In." What did you say? What do you mean, "there's a crack in the light"?"

Student 7: Psychoanalyst, author.

"In Bion, there is a strange formalism, references to scientific deductive systems and The Grid. At first I took it on a kind of psychoanalytic faith that it was worth persevering to get to the core of it. It would be too easy to say that I persevered and finally "got it." The truth is more that I found a way of being more comfortable in my oscillations between Paranoid–Schizoid and Depressive Positions, between what became after a long time a kind of love for Bion and a persistent discomfort before a writing that often remains opaque and alien. But gradually, I found my way to Bion's own voice, not the poetic jazz beat improvisational rhythms of Eigen but a different kind of music, an elegantly stark mathematical minimalism. Still, if not for Eigen's classes I would have given up.

"I remember one class, Eigen working on a section from *Cogitations*. He starts by reading an excerpt:

The patient comes to the door and looks away to avoid my eyes. He is dirty and unkempt; he wears gloves but they are not a pair. His face expresses almost physical pain. He holds out his hand limply to allow it to be shaken, but he seems almost to dissociate himself from the act physically as well as mentally. He lies down on the couch. "Well", he says, "I don't seem to have much to say." (p. 218)

"Eigen does not rush forward to get to the essence of the case, doesn't grab for psychological landmarks, familiar constructions to bolster our sense of our own analytic sharpness. Eigen goes slow, savoring the essence of what is being described. He repeats phrases, 'he holds out his hand limply to allow it to be shaken.' Now we must pause before this limp hand, we must hold the limp hand, hold the dissociated holding. There is a timelessness about the account as if the patient has always been there, offering his hand, saying very little and Bion has always been there, observing this moment, seeing the pain on the patient's face, feeling the limpness of that hand. Eigen takes in Bion's account with the same slow, precise caution as Bion takes in the patient. There is nowhere to go, the sense of timelessness characteristic of intellectual immersion and fascination mixes with the timelessness of the psychotic state. We have to hold the tension, the wish to hold and the wish to dissociate.

"Later in the same passage, Bion writes, 'In short, I cannot have as much confidence in my ability to tell the reader what happened as I have in my ability to do something to the reader that I have had done to me. I have had an emotional experience; I feel confident in my ability to recreate that emotional experience, but not to represent it' (p. 219). Eigen as teacher of Bion, is true to this focus. Something that was done to Bion was done to Eigen. The words of this vignette, now read in class, may now again cause something to be done in all of us. I remember a question, a classmate challenging Bion's assumptions, his authoritative role as the analyst confident in his own impressions of the psychotic patient. But Eigen is not swayed to respond or think in these terms. He doesn't say much but tries to stay situated at the moment of impact, to tolerate the seemingly meaningless flow of a session that seems like an excerpt from a Beckett play. For a moment the disembodied disturbance of the patient in the vignette seems present in the class. It is hard to know what is happening. Nobody is writing notes. We try to take in what is happening."

Student 8: Recent institute graduate, found Bion through her supervisor and became a Bion reader. Took my institute seminars and entered my private seminar in the past few years, hopes to teach soon. I have always been impressed by her knowledge of *A Memoir of the Future* and her feel for poetry.

> "Bion has entered my psyche in bits and pieces. Sometimes the bits are a digestible amount, like an infant's happy feed; sometimes more than I can handle, like shrapnel from a mortar burst. I have learned Bion from the dialectic between sitting in Bion seminars and sitting in analytic sessions, deepening attunement to shock waves.
>
> "Learning to read Bion is learning to read slowly, deeply, word for word. Chewing cuds. This translates into deeper listening in sessions.

Letting words have impact. Learning the language of impact and catastrophe. Leaving room for the impact of silence too.

"The image of Bion emerging from the slaughter of World War I has stayed with me and often crops up in sessions, alerting me to deep trauma, ghosts and murder in the room. A wounded soul emerging amidst a gray fog, a fog I have learned to sit with."

Student 9: Took an institute course on Bion with me a year or two ago and recently joined my private seminar. Had been reading Bion and Kleinians for a long time. A special interest was severe, chronic depression.

"I began reading Bion, the Kleinians and post-Kleinians in the 1990s and found them enormously helpful in making intellectual sense of what I have been up against clinically and personally. Your contribution for me has been to bring emotion/feeling (feeling matters!) into the picture. When you describe the real frailty of the psychic apparatus to do the work that it is supposed to, to manage the emotional floods of intense affect, I can begin to find some space for feeling, compassion, empathy, rather than judgment in the face of my own frustration, rage, anxiety, sadness, and at times hopelessness. This leads to a very different position in relation to the work both with the patient and with myself. What previously was understood as a refusal to suffer can now be understood and responded to as an inability to suffer."

She referred to Bion's idea of developing a capacity to suffer *vs.* evasion of suffering, sensing in an earlier intellectual stance subtle distancing or "blame" attached to evasion when emphasis was placed on the patient's "refusal". Pressure began to lift when she thought more in terms of working with incapacity and, if possible, gradually helping to build capacity, a ground for compassion and care. A subtle but important shift of attitude.

Student 10: Took institute classes with me more than a decade ago and now teaches Bion, among other writers, at institutes, presents at conferences, and writes papers.

"I've experienced group euphoria in a classroom when we read Bion's remark, 'The psychoanalyst should aim at achieving a state of mind so that at every session he feels he has not seen the patient before. If he feels he has, he is treating the wrong patient'.

"A typical question:

"Student: 'What do I say to the patient who stormed out of the office, slamming the door when, or if, he comes back next session?'

"Teacher: 'How about "hello"?'

"Student: 'Really? I don't have to analyze the meltdown from last session?'

"Teacher: 'The patient (personality part) who returned to see you may not be the same patient (personality part) who could not bear being with you. If the same part returns, he'll let you know he's there and what to say can start to evolve.'"

Student 11: Long-time reader of Bion and my work, as well as many related writers, for example, Grotstein, Ferro, Meltzer. He attended a few of my seminars when I gave events in his city or he visited mine. Psychoanalyst, writer, teacher.

"Teaching Bion is an oxymoron. You can't really teach Bion. I believe you can commit to a process of exploring Bion's work, of getting-to-know the variety of problems he posed for the practicing psychoanalyst. Getting-to-know Bion is like getting to know any wilderness. You have to return to that place over and over again and begin to live there. Things don't stand still. You start to have many new impressions that arise at levels you never noticed before. At best you can be a guide a little way into the wilderness, but there are no experts.

"You can share the emotional impact of states Bion points to and become interested in experiences others have and how they think about them. Getting to know Bion helps ground you as well as crack you, helps you to develop courage."

Student 12: Long-time seminar member. Psychotherapist, Buddhist, incorporates body work. She tries to express what a Bion seminar hour feels like for her.

"I walk in, heart settles, breath slows, my edges expand, another world emerges. The human constructs of time and space blend/bleed, warmth flows as I relax. There is no separation between teacher, subject and student, all are possible. Intuition ignites, mind wonders through dreams and associations. Willingness to be present grows word by word. Reading, speaking, we tumble out loud. We find vectors that reach, threads that get tangled or unbound, secret joy of the endless. There is a daring sense of freedom to explore the darkest, unspeakable corners, playing in the sometimes graspable innermost thinking, feeling being of Bion. The hour is over, I leave, elated, exhausted, full. Gratitude pours through me as I walk back to my office."

Student 13: What she sent me is too long to quote but I wish to mention her as her history is different from others here. She began with Bion's group work in the 1970s, doing Bion-derived groups in a university setting, helping to train businessmen. Since then, she used a Bion-based group model for problems that arise in her own university classrooms. She applied Bion to individual and group work with addicts, who may, in part, use drugs in lieu of missing or diminished psychic functions. She began reading my work in the 1980s, which added emphasis on the work of faith, catastrophic processes, and wounded capacities to sustain and process experience. Since we live very far from each other, she has not been in my seminars, except for one meeting when she came to New York, yet our paths crossed psychically through shared interests.

Student 14: Psychoanalyst, teacher. Studied Bion with me fourteen years. Has strong interest in the interface of Bion, Wittgenstein, and Buddhism:

"I think of the passage in Cogitations (pp. 234–235) in which Bion distinguishes between two kinds of problems, those 'where an emotional experience . . . is secondary to a problem that awaits solution' and those 'in which the emotional experience itself is the problem.' Of the first, 'it is possible to regard the problem as one of unrelated objects requiring synthesis.' However, with regard to the second, 'there is probably no way of regarding the problem "as" anything at all.' I recall several meetings of our Bion group that were spent in the vicinity of this powerful remark.

"What seems striking centers around the use of 'no' here. No way of regarding the problem as anything at all. No way. Here something is different. In the one instance, there is a way; here there is none. We are left, as it were, looking into space. We come up against our desire to see something, to proceed one way, but that way vanishes before us. Now we are someplace different. To find our way about here is to bear this 'no way.' When we think of the centrality for Bion of bearing emptiness, bearing the 'no-thing,' of the way in which this 'patience' (PS) with the no-thing is a condition for thought, we are struck that *we* have been brought *in this moment* to such a place, brought to feel it from the inside."

Rather than elaborate on the above student–teacher sketches related to learning, teaching, or using Bion, I will let them speak for themselves. One thread I want to mention is the paradox of how uplifting it can be to be released to go to the darkest or unknown places. To be able to sit in emotional darkness and find patience, endurance, care, and love even in frustration, hate, impatience, and hopelessness stimulates possible growth of a new kind of capacity, partly involving creative waiting, intuitive sensing, letting psyche speak or grunt or weep or rip. Hidden ecstasy runs through psychic life, as does catastrophic destructiveness (Eigen, 2001). Too often, the two are fused and indistinguishable. It is, perhaps, in the domain of indistinguishable unknowns that Bion's dogged perseverance in face of everything is most striking and encouraging.

Some notes I received, but omitted here because of space considerations, wrote of class-work as dream-work and Bion writing of sessions as dream-work, dreaming the patient, dreaming the analyst, dreaming each other into being. I think of a remark he made related to a patient: "I am his other self and it is called a dream" (*Cogitations*, p. 186). Much work goes on at a level that might be described as dream to dream.

By way of ending this chapter, I would like to add a few notes on Bion's writings on love. He depicts domains of love ranging from murderous love to love of God. For Bion, emotions are, or can be, violent (1994, pp. 249–250). Love is violent as well as hate and the emotional spectrum that grows out of their fusions. Their violence may increase as a function of deficiency of sustaining and processing capacity, to the point where love can become cruel. Not all love and hate are cruel, but can become so. Increased cruelty goes with decreasing concern for other subjects, truth, and life.

Murderous love in itself may or may not be cruel. He gives as example (1994, p. 372), "A lioness nuzzles and shows every sign of feelings of love and affection . . . for prey it has destroyed; but it is love that destroys the loved object". Destructive love often plays a role in the lives of those who come to us for help (Eigen, 1999, 2001). In some, cruelty as well. And yet, Bion says, there is love we have no words for, something touched perhaps by phrases like "love of God". I think of Spinoza's "*amor Dei*" and Greek *agape*. About this love Bion writes,

> This other love, vaguely adumbrated, vaguely foreshadowed in human speech, is of an entirely different character; it is not simply a quantitative difference in the kind of love one animal has for another or which the baby has for the breast. It is the further extension of 'absolute love', which cannot be described in the terms of sensuous reality or experience. For that there has to be a language of infra-sensuous or ultra-sensuous, something that lies outside the spectrum of sensuous experience and articulate language. (1994, p. 372)

A love, he suggests, that precipitates a crises of faith in face of violent love. A crises of faith that lifts existence.

CHAPTER SEVEN

Variants of mystical participation

Mystical participation. Is it a state that underlies experience? Can we better say it is a dimension of experience or sets of dimensions, rather than situate it below–above or earlier–later? What you and I might mean by mystical or participation or related terms might not be the same. I am not sure what I mean, but loosely refer to something sensed. It may occur in varied affective keys: dread, awe, love, heaven, hell, joy, ecstasy, horror, hope, hate. Yes, there are hate frenzies, hate ecstasies, hate unions. Destructive as well as creative mystical participations (Eigen, 2001). There are those who say that destructive union is part of creativeness.

Dimensions—plural. Mystics speak of going through many doors, worlds, gates. Beatrice in Dante's heaven goes from one heaven through another. Heaven keeps opening. Invagination is often an implied image. In my early twenties, after a physical intervention by a somatic therapist, he asked how I felt and I spoke the truth: "I feel like a vagina." My whole body became vaginal. His paranoid aspect came to the fore and said, "How do you know how a vagina feels?" At that moment, in my experience, I was one.

A vaginal self, a vaginal body. A Lacanian might say imaginary vagina. One could give a gender analysis and rake me over the coals for my biases. What can I say? In my mind, my body—vagina. Hallucination? Can the body hallucinate? Yes, it can. Was it hallucinating then? At the moment, I didn't care. It was wonderful.

Winnicott (1953) speaks of positive aspects of illusion and puts in that category much art and religious experience. Beneficial, enriching illusions. Not at all divorced from truth. They enlarge the domain of emotional or perceptual truth. In my case, to experience my body that way stayed with me the rest of my life. More—it opened a gate of experiencing that has grown since then. Once touched, such moments make you aware of possibilities that can undergo development.

Also in my early twenties, doubled over in pain on a bus, I found myself going deeper and deeper into the intensity until I began to black out. The blackout became more total and I lost usual consciousness. I would say, simply, I lost consciousness, which comes close to what I felt, but I must guess that I was not entirely unconscious. Something was conscious. I did not fall over on to the floor. I remained glued to the experience, part of it, in it, held and encompassed by it, penetrating it. How can these contrasting images—penetrating and encompassing be happening at once—are they not contradictory? In emotional life, they go together, they are one or, at moments, can be one.

And then the unexpected. I should say the even more unexpected, because none of this was expected. The blackness opened to Light. The pain was permeated by Light. Heavenly Light. Through the pain, the darkness, Light. One of the most basic archetypes, at work everywhere. But thoughts like that were far from what I was feeling. I felt only a miracle, the most intense pain an opening to Light. It had very much an effect like my body becoming vaginal. Light permeated, suffused psyche–soma, through me, through my pores, cells, nerves. It permeated my I. The aftermath was a sense of Faith.

All through my professional career I have been describing such moments. The sequence, in one or another of its variants, I call a rhythm of faith (e.g., 1992, 2004, 2009, 2010, 2011a,b, 2012a). In therapy it is a kind of going through, coming through something together. Perhaps going through something that went wrong between us. Every session, in some way, a crisis of faith.

A sense of mysterious connection takes many forms. Herbert Read (1965) describes such a possibility in caveman drawings of animals. He describes a possible link between hunter and hunted, the latter drawn with beauty and grace, oneness between killer and killed that includes and transcends death. In Judaism, one's blessing of food elevates the latter, raises soul of food, as does lighting a candle commemorating a close one's death, raising the loved one's soul higher. Something sacred in physical and spiritual nourishment.

Again in my twenties, I once stood for hours in Golden Gate Park entranced with a hyena in the zoo. We could not stop our eye contact, staring into each other's eyes. What were we feeling? Fear? Attraction? Fascination? How could such different beings as we be tied to each other, total strangers, no context? I would not exactly call this merger uplifting, certainly not solely uplifting. I was left, too, with a sense of puzzlement. Who were we, what were we doing, what were we asking, seeking, giving, withholding? Yet, there was a definite rise of intensity that captured us both. We could not let go until fatigue let us go.

Maybe a year later, back in New York, I was going to Philadelphia with a young lady who had a crush on me. I was going to play a gig in a band and she felt like coming. Again, unexpectedly, eye-lock happened, this time human eyes, glued, caught. We gave into it. Melded. I do not think I was totally melded, but our eyes were absorbed, absorbing each other. It spread through my skin, a sense of absorption, rapt. We stayed like that all the way to Philadelphia and all the way back. I did not know what it was, what was happening. She smiled, "You don't know? We're meshed." Meshing—it felt like an enlightenment ray. She seemed to know the territory and guided me.

You probably can describe many moments of being taken out of yourself, heightened moments of beauty, wonder, love, or dread. It is a very precious capacity that threads through and uplifts living. It can, too, be decimating, as in the mysticism of war, or psychosis, or evil. A kind of free-floating capacity that can attach to many subjects in many ways (Eigen, 1993, 1998, 2001).

Reflecting on the above experiences and others not mentioned here, I want to say that they happened to someone, they happened to me. I might have been lost or semi-lost in experiencing, but someone was there experiencing. I would not say this comes close to being a loss of self in God. Yet, something beyond usual boundaries happened, some kind of interpenetration, interweaving, opening.

In the case of pain opening to Light, it was as if the very intensity of the pain perforated the psyche, opening another dimension. The Light itself beauteous, life giving. An unexpected intimacy with an aspect of the Most Intimate of All. A kind of oneness, yes, but not without me. Similarly, transforming into a vaginal body or surrendering to intermeshing mutual eye-absorption, I was there, but more than I was happening. I was learning in my own way, at the time a very secular way, something about "I yet not I". Secular me was opening to a More of Life, a sense of numinous, yet just plain me happening. Life as mystery and down to earth.

As time went on and I became a psychotherapist, I learnt more about the variety and possibilities of such experiences from my patients and began to grapple with saying something that might do a little justice to what was happening. My attempts inevitably came up short and echoed other writers concerned with double capacity, especially capacity to unite and distinguish, a capacity or state that works in many ways on many levels. Among the many writers I liked: Balint's (1968) interpenetrating harmonious mixup; Matte-Blanco's (1988) symmetrical–asymmetrical modes of being; Werner's (1948) syncretic experiencing; Elkin's (1958–1959, 1972) primordial consciousness and primordial self-awareness; Barfield's (1984) intuitive and analytic aspects of mind; Bohm's (1980) implicate–explicate orders, and other varied works on sensory–perceptual–somatic experiencing and more.

One formulation I came up with, trying to stay close to my own and patients' experience, involves a distinction–union structure. That is, I posited a structure in which distinction and union elements both play a role, a kind of DNA–RNA of experience, both tendencies always present in varying kinds of relationship. Now there might be more distinction, now more union, one background or foreground for the other. As structural components, they enter in variable relations with each other: fused, antagonistic, reversible, oscillating, synchronous, indistinguishable, extremes, symbiotic, co-nourishing. Each thread has its biography and the two as a whole make up the biography of the over-arching structure they are parts of. Distinction–union as a structure made up of sub-structures, complex structural processes at work (1986, 1992, 2011b, 2012a,b).

The first time I became aware of this in a dramatic way with a patient was early in my practice (1973, 2011b, 2012b). He was a severely alcoholic man who binged and might wake in the street days later not knowing where he was. He did well in Alcoholics Anonymous but needed more. The combination of AA and therapy did the trick. We were together a long time and went through many things. The particular turning point I have in mind began with him gradually withdrawing from life, holing up in his apartment. This contraction happened over time and became very scary for both of us. As a young therapist, I wondered what I was doing wrong. Was I provoking a suicide, a breakdown? Would my nascent practice end before it began? Therapy was a huge contrast with his upbringing and much of his life, which had been chaotic, explosive. A raging, impulsive, alcoholic father and a mother for whom everything was too much. Was the quiet of therapy driving him crazy? But something in me said sit with it, go with it. If I had to locate this sense, it was a kind of umbilical sensation, contact I feared was imaginary. It is not that I did not speak. I was a friendly, caring background presence. I said and did what I could. But the intensity of the withdrawal that sucked him in was silencing.

One day, unexpectedly, he reported a turn, an experience that frightened but touched and lifted him. In his aloneness, he was drawn deeper and deeper into an alone point that became his I turning into a radiant point. He could not believe what was happening, a radiant I, an inner I-light. It came with a sense of peace, tranquillity, which did not end his inner turbulence but added something new to his life-feeling. After more weeks, the radiant I expanded to encompass Everything, radiance Everywhere. It felt miraculous. The Light permeating inner–outer reality. His drinking stopped. There was no further binging. His everyday life expanded as well. Before he left therapy, he began to live with his girlfriend, making future plans. She was someone he met in AA.

What happened, I wondered? I knew the Light existed, but to come into therapy in unanticipated ways and be decisive? One way I have come to look at it is that inadvertently I provided a background presence that enabled emergence of a quiet his life failed to provide (2009, Chapters One and Two, 2011b, Chapters One and Two). A quiet deep in the self instead of maddening noise chronically ripping him apart.

We felt lucky, my patient and I, entering a process we knew nothing of and discovering it had its own unfolding. Since then, I have found that freeing moments can come in limitless ways. In *The Psychoanalytic Mystic* (1998), I write of mystical experience involving shatter, sensation, self, other, no-self, God, no-God, difference, union, between, emptiness. Sometimes, I call it free-floating radiance. In my patient's case, it took a particular form that worked for him. I have heard from others, now nearly fifty years later, that he has led a good life, a hard but full life, rich with experience.

As I have lived and learnt more, I am aware of the fertile I-point as a point of radiance: I am I, I am what I will be, I am, I am that I am, I yet not I, I am that . . . add your favourite locution for this centre of experience. Is it the only centre? Of course not. The deepest centre?

A question such as the last makes me think of *Kabbalah*, one of the great light shows in spiritual history. Concealed and manifest light, concealed of the concealed, mystery of mysteries. Layering of dimensions expressed as limitless One, Infinite beyond number, light so light it is seen as darkness, darkness so dark it is seen as light, nothingness–emptiness. You might say, like Freud's libido taking many forms via displacements, radiance takes many forms as part of creative work. One might also say we are speaking of what is beyond conception, words, and images. There are passages in *Kabbalah* that call "it" *what, that, not, negative existence*, as well as *my cup runneth over*. Nearly all mystics speak of going beyond opposites, binaries, where dark and light are one as well as dark and light.

I want to share something from my recent practice: a patient who had been ill for many years and was approaching death. When she came to me, she feared dying as young as her mother, who passed away in her forties from disabling muscular degeneration. My patient had lupus much of her adult life and, as she got older, other serious illnesses developed as well. Now that death was imminent at the age of seventy, she feared dying in a tormented state that would last all eternity. Religious teachings that influenced her dogmatised that your last state was the state you would be in forever. I do not share this belief. I feel faith is deeper than belief systems. This brought her some relief, but she still dreaded dying in a tormented state, whether or not it lasted forever.

She had come near death many times (I write of some of her experiences in 2004, pp. 85–104), but now the feeling mounted. In her last two weeks, I began speaking about the *yechida* soul. In Kabbalah–Chassidus there are at least five soul levels or dimensions, probably infinities of infinities of dimensions. *Nefesh* is the "animal" or vital soul, characteristic of our earth world, our space–time life (the tenth *Sephirah, Malchut*). *Ruach* (breath, spirit) we will call an emotional soul, spanning lower and higher emotions (*Sephirot* 5–9). *Neshama* is a higher soul, involving wisdom, understanding, knowledge (*Sephirot* 2–3 plus *Daat*, a hidden dimension). One might see these as intellect, although I tend to see them allied, too, with intuition, A fourth soul is *Chaya*, life, which involves a profound faith dimension, straddling the first *sephirah* (*Keter*, divine will, creative nothingness, humility, faith) and infinity. You might roughly compare these with Jung's four functions, sensation, feeling, intellect, intuition. Or Husserl's empirical ego, psychological ego, and transcendental ego. There are many parallels linking with ancient mysteries (Orpheus, Apollo, Egyptian and Tibetan Books of the Dead), Plato, Aristotle—you can add your favourites.

Chassidus notes a fifth, still higher soul dimension, *yechida*, in which one's essence is one with God's essence. It is this last dimension I appealed to in the face of my patient's torment.

She was a profound Kabbalah student and teacher and knew immediately what I meant when I said go higher, touch *yechida*, live in *yechida*. She began feeling profound relief almost immediately and we maintained contact. She already knew I did not feel one stayed in a state of torment for eternity, if that was one's last state. But now I was asking her to let *yechida* lift her above the storm, above the torment. In what was to be our last talk, I was supporting her soul rising towards *yechida*, making contact with *yechida*, living with and in *yechida*. We both felt it happening. She died before our next scheduled phone session at ease and in a peaceful state.

I knew of the healing effects of *yechida* contact from my own experience, but whether or not it would have that resonance with my patient I did not know. I felt impelled to share *yechida* life with her. It was not a wilful decision or thought. I felt it coming up, pressing for expression, and took the chance, whether out of desperation or love. Again, luck, grace—she took to it like a duck to water, as if these were words she was waiting to hear. An area of freedom waiting to open.

There is a time for constant struggle, to go through things from the bottom up. But there is also a time to rise above it all, to reach the highest point, beyond one's torment and turbulence. There are roots above as well as below. I love a scene from *The Gospel at Colonus*, the Sophocles drama played by gospel singers in 1985 at the Brooklyn Academy of Music. Oedipus seemed to rise from his own grave, from the lowest of lowest points, while the singers repeated, "Higher! Higher! Higher!" He rose above the hells, the self-persecution—free for that moment. A moment of grace in which torments fade away. We rise from our graves, higher than our hells.

At the beginning of a Kabbalah and Psychoanalysis seminar last week, I gave a guided meditation, going into wisdom (*Chochma*, the second *sephirah*). Everyone was sitting quietly. One sentence I said was something like: "At this moment, you can do nothing wrong." A few days later one of the participants told me she felt a weight lift when she heard those words, a release, a shell open. Something that had been tight around her, constricting, strangulating, gave way. At this moment you can do nothing wrong.

The word "yechida" has to do with one. One God. The One that is All, whether you name it God or nothing or That or Cosmos or . . . Near the end of the Jewish service there is a song that says of God: "There is none else". In this there is a sense of unity beyond difference, perhaps a more widespread experience than is realised. It informs everyday life, I feel, binding it together. There are so many ways to turn these phrases: one in many, many in one, unity beyond difference, difference in unity. There is also an urge and, at times, capacity to go beyond all of these terms into the termless, the thing itself, what Bion writes as O, unknowable, ultimate, infinite reality: "The fundamental reality is 'infinity', the unknown, the situation for which there is no language – not even one borrowed by the artist or the religious – which gets anywhere near to describing it" (1994, p. 372).

There are people who live their lives at a lower flame level, sometimes feeling they are missing something. They have moments when seas part, but quickly close, or are far and few between. One senses the reality of mystical participation, and the meaning this can bring, by its absence. One patient, affable, a bit sardonic, able to poke holes in just about everyone and everything, complains about a tepid existence. I like him and he me, but we sense a kind of chronic background depression draining life urges. He tells me he has not been able to hold jobs. He puts the latter down and leaves. His current job has been the longest lasting. He explains that he has been able to control his provocative, grandiose streak better. Lately, there might even be hints of moments his wife and he try to communicate rather than talk past each other.

He feels he has always had to dampen feeling, play it down, afraid of aliveness. Yet, he has moments—camping, boating, working with his hands. I find his ideas interesting. He has good insights into plays, sees things others might not, but there is a deprecating quality in his tone. Deprecating both towards self and other.

"It started at home as a child, being alone. If I showed interest in something, both my parents put me down, ridiculed, made fun of excitement. I learned to hold back, stay more by myself. As I grew. this turned into a habit of lying low, not going too far or doing too much. As I got older, I began to realise that I was afraid of creativity, not able to sustain intensity. Creative or sexual intensity. I think I had the feeling that acting leads to death." He noted this was a theme in ancient and modern literature, an association of desire, action, and death: what you think will bring fulfilment brings disaster, or merely disappointment.

He had interests and, although he did not hold most jobs long, found other ways of doing well enough on his own. Life is not without its pleasures. But moments that ring the bell—he felt his bell was starved for ringing.

His heart opened completely when he had a grandchild. He was proud of and loved his son—but his grandson! The deliciousness of life touched him fully. His whole face and demeanour changed when speaking about the time spent taking care of him. The deprecation and low-burner attitude were gone. His being became a heart smile. I have seen this with many parents and their children and sometimes more so with grandparents. Their life opens to a new dimension. I tend to see in this a mystical participation aspect that lightens life. A kind of implicit mystical dimension in everyday life. The taste of fuller heart life he has with his grandchild contrasts with more tepid existence otherwise—not completely, but makes him aware something is missing, that there could and should be more. He feels there could be more but is too afraid to let it happen.

In a seemingly opposite situation, a woman I work with goes from one peak experience to another. She also suffers the dull interim of boring existence, aspects of her job and family life. She came in contact with a guru who lit her up, made her ecstatic, so much so she began resenting her everyday life and began thinking of breaking it up. She feels life is inherently ecstatic and she should be in ecstasy most or all of the time. She uses ecstasy as a criterion for judging the rest of her life, and finds the latter wanting.

Luckily, both of us now feel, she withstood her guru's advances and did not forsake her real family life for his cosmic promise. Yet, she felt what he promised was real and life would be empty and unreal without it. I mainly stayed in the middle ground, keeping possibilities open. Perhaps she sensed a tension in my attitude enabling her to feel I "got" her situation, at least somewhat. I valued ecstasy, too. At the same time, her guru seemed something of a loose wire, sleeping with students as part of the enlightenment journey, cosmic openness to where the Spirit led. I felt my patient to be in a whirlwind, blown by the winds of highs and lows, her feelings fanned by the guru's moods, alternating between promise and abandonment. She was riding the wild horse of her emotional life bareback and it hurt. When she drew back into her family, the guru scolded her for betraying a greater calling. But staying with the Great Call through him was like sticking her head in a meat grinder.

A breakthrough came by chance or grace, reading the early part of my book, *Kabbalah and Psychoanalysis*, where I spoke about loving God with all one's heart and soul and might. And passages in which I recounted how the words, "I love you", would come from nowhere and I would say them over and over. She found herself saying them over and over, too, and felt God saying, "I love you." They said "I love you" to each other repeatedly. At least for a time, something ignited in her. The words, "I love you", represented a kind of match igniting her inner love of God and a sense of God's love for her. She was trying to reach this dimension of feeling through the guru, a domain of experiencing intrinsic to her being. She now contacted it within.

The road ahead will not be easy, but something began to fall into place. Her husband and children looked good to her once more and daily life felt alive. The ups and downs and extremes of intensity continue, but is something of a way of life. How they function and are used, whether they can be sources of enrichment or sink a life, is in balance. A few days ago, between sessions, I received the following note:

> "You speak of Nachman talking about the Heart being in everything [Rabbi Nachman of Bratslav, in *Kabbalah and Psychoanalysis*, 2012a Chapter Two]. I also recently discovered the truth of Ramana Maharshi's words that it is all one Heart, beating—expanding and

contracting, inhaling and exhaling. A rhythmic opening and closing of life as it unfolds. Much like our experiences of up and down, of happiness and despair. A day full of joy and bliss followed by a night thick with pain and suffering.

"It all began to make sense to pay attention to our breath, to stay with it for it is that same rhythm. May we be more open to this breath of life—inhale and exhale till our last breath."

I think of the psalm, "I go to sleep weeping and wake up laughing". Who knows where this journey will take us, how the threads will play out? She is fighting for her life, not any life, but one that is maximally worthwhile on the one hand, and one that is livable on the other. Is Winnicott's "good enough" good enough? I think of Winnicott's prayer, "Oh God, may I be alive when I die!"

"May I be alive when I die!" Alive and dying—heightened conjunction and transcendence of opposites. One could go further: dying as one of the great experiences of a lifetime. We note the conjunction of dying and orgasm in the language of Eros, dying fused with heightened intensity. A fusion reflected in opera, theatre, and art, a thread that runs through culture. On a lesser scale, real enough for me at the time, in younger years kissing a girl I felt so much for, and as we kissed I felt faint, I was going to pass out, no, I was going to die. I murmured, "I'm dying, I'm dying." She responded, "Not yet. We need you." I was beyond happy.

This morning I spoke with a dying woman I care for deeply. She has not spoken for days after a stroke. She answered my hi with a faltering hi. I told her I love her from the deepest place in my heart, that she is beautiful, that it is going to be beautiful, all beauty. She tried to say, "I love you", but could not organise sounds into words. She stopped trying to speak and answered with a full heart smile. I felt the lack in our goodbye, such a loss, permanent, forever. And yet, such a glow. I think, too, of *Tiferet*, the centre of the Kabbalah Tree of Life: Beauty. The heart of the Tree of Life spreading in all directions.

Sometimes, I call mystical participation oneness thinking, oneness experiencing. Two are in it, three, multiplicity. Distinction in union, union in distinction. Co-union, communion. One and All. You and me and all of us leaves of the Tree of Life, sometimes branches, roots. The mystery of individual identity in All-ness, a basic structure of being.

I wish to close with telling the story of Rabbi Shimon bar Yohai's (Shimon, son of Yohai) death, as depicted in the *Zohar* (Liebes, 1993; Mathers, 1887; Matt, 2009). Some Chassidic groups celebrate Rabbi Shimon as the *Zohar's* author, roughly around 150 CE. A story is that he and his son, Rabbi Eliezar, hid in a cave for thirteen years studying and meditating and there the seeds of the *Zohar* were sown. Scholars place authorship in the thirteenth century by Moses de Leon of Spain, although others also may have contributed to the book we now have. We can spend a lot of space pulling out diverse views of authorship and motivation. It is said Moses de Leon chose to attribute authorship to Rabbi Shimon so the book would be taken more seriously and perhaps gain more currency and sales. The *Zohar*—Radiance—was written in idiosyncratic Aramaic, as if it came from long ago, and when scholars came for the original manuscript at Moses de Leon's death, his wife said, "Here it is. He made it all up." Is this work or series of works a great literary hoax? A spiritual masterpiece? A mystical journey or mythic adventure? It is possible all of these currents are mixed and that Rabbi Shimon and other characters served as vehicles to evoke and channel a human sense of divine mystery.

In a previous convocation, Rabbi Shimon and his companions took turns discoursing on hidden mysteries. It was felt the time had come to make them public, perhaps a sense of the Messiah's imminence. Three of the companions could not survive the intensity and perished. The remaining ones now convened on Rabbi Shimon's death day. Unlike the previous convocation, on this day only Rabbi Shimon would speak. He felt it necessary to unburden himself of remaining divine secrets, perhaps the most secret of all, so as to enter the world to come without shame. His son, Rabbi Eliezar, would recite the words Rabbi Shimon spoke, while Rabbi Abba wrote and kept a record, and the others meditate.

At the earlier convocation, Rabbi Shimon felt something missing. He felt himself an incomplete person and expressed this by calling himself unmarried. In actual, earthly existence, he was married with children, one of them, Rabbi Eliezar, who was in attendance and participating in that very moment. Rabbi Shimon felt, rather, an imperfect, incomplete and defective man because of something lacking in his marriage to the spiritual bride, the *Shechinah*, a feminine aspect of God associated with the tenth *sephirah*, *Malchut* (Eigen,

2012a). A spiritual defect—not married to God fully enough, not married to the *Shechinah* fully enough. So, today, his death day, was his marriage day. And the *Shechinah's* kiss, a culmination of his spiritual life, would be the moment of his death.

What was missing would be found, the defect rectified, marriage of the soul with Godly Presence. Kiss of life one with kiss of death, offspring of earthly–heavenly, inner male–female union. Dying in the *Shechinah's* embrace, the acme of life. Indeed, his last word was "Life".

Recently, a founder of Apple computers, Steve Jobs, died, and it is said his last word was "Wow!" I do not mean to put Steve Jobs and Rabbi Shimon on the same spiritual level. Also, Jobs was a real person and while Rabbi Shimon lived and died two thousand years ago, the death scene in the *Zohar* is a fiction made up perhaps one thousand years ago. Life. Wow! What life was opening as Rabbi Shimon was dying? What soul life was opening for the writer who envisioned this?

There is much to be said about Rabbi Shimon's last discourse that we cannot bring out here. As he said, the whole day was his, and he said almost everything he could. What was he speaking about the moment that he died? The Light of Lights. There is concealed light, the concealed of the concealed, yet light manifests as well. The ten *sephirot* are semi-manifested lights, all with unmanifest aspects. The *sephirot* are channels of creation. In human terms, creative capacities and states. But in the *Zohar*, they are Godly realities through which creation emanates. All the lights, *sephirot*, channels, and capacities are part of One Light, the Godly of Godly lights, unknown, unrevealed, hidden. More—not only are they all parts of Godly light, they are that light itself. We feel the limitless light and all the light channels not just spoken about, but manifestly present in Rabbi Shimon's final moment. Separate, yet not separate, distinct and interlacing and one—lit up as far as human capacity can bear light, limited and limitless, emanating from a source that eludes manifest knowing, a source giving rise to intimations, implicit contact.

"There is none else." Only God. God is all there is.

In the silence that followed, Rabbi Abba realised that Rabbi Shimon had passed, lying on his right side, smiling.

We are invited to participate in divine mystery. We feel what must be one of the greatest light shows ever reverberating through our beings. We are part of the lights, yet in tears, appreciative of divine currents working in us. We put all our bad things into this infinite light matrix and let it do its work. What is it we feel? A sense of the holy? Something no words or thoughts circumscribe? A sense of the Most Intimate of All touching us?

CHAPTER EIGHT

No one can save you from the work that you have to do on yourself*

First, I read Michael Eigen. His was like no other writing I had yet encountered on the inner life of psychoanalytic thinkers. He wrote about therapy from the point of view of a therapist participating fully, with heart and soul, in the frustrating process of psychotherapy in which time flows forwards and backwards, until tiny points of transparency, incremental miracles, appear in the seemingly impenetrable armour of life.

I have always been suspicious of psychoanalysis's reductive instincts—in English slang, therapists are called "shrinks", and for good reason. Analysts, it seemed to me, want to kiss us and turn us into frogs, reveal reality as a war of instinctual urges, in which every desire is also a naked grab for power, and every strategy conceals an erection.

In Eigen's writing, there is room for everything except reduction— or escape. In *The Psychoanalytic Mystic* (1998), he shows us the traces

---

* The original interview by Micha Odenheimer in *Eretz Acheret* added the subtitle, "About the spirituality branded in the intimate encounters of human suffering". The interview begins with Micha Odenheimer saying a few words about reading Eigen's work.

of mystical experience, like suspended particles of gold dust, which can be seen at the margins of the great psychoanalytic theories, as if out of the corners of our eye, at the place where language and subjectivity have collided. Understanding is always born of ecstasy, he says, and ecstasy of the yearning for something unnamable, towards which we are drawn like moths to a candle, like mystics to God (Eigen, 2001).

Unnameable, and yet present, right here, right now, nowhere if not in the person sitting across from us—parent, child, friend or, in the examples he skilfully burns on to the pages of his books, those seeking psychological healing. The healing takes place, he tells us, when life meets life, the life of the therapist and that of the patient mingling, tiny beads of meaning condensing into dew drops small enough to be absorbed through a lifetime of defences, pure enough to nourish new life.

After reading Eigen (though not yet enough), I meet him, in his office on Central Park West, facing the snow-covered park. In the outer room are unruly stacks of books, including *Toxic Nourishment*, *Rage*, *Ecstasy*, *The Psychoanalytic Mystic*, *The Sensitive Self*, and *Emotional Storm*. Eigen is one of the most prominent psychoanalysts working in America today: associate adjunct professor at New York University's Post-Doctoral Program in Psychotherapy and Psychoanalysis, senior analyst and faculty member, the National Psychological Association for Psychoanalysis, and former editor in chief of *The Psychoanalytic Review*, which has been publishing continuously since 1913.

The inner room, where his therapy sessions take place, is small and intimate. At sixty-nine, Eigen seems considerably younger. He is unobtrusively masculine, speaks with authority yet with respect for the listener, his voice textured with experience, with the roughness of the Jewish New York of a half century ago, tempered by a lifetime of fascination with far away cultures and religions and close encounters with human suffering. Without the slightest air of analytic distance or superiority born of age, status, or intellectual powers, we begin to speak.

Micha: I'm interested in your history in terms of religion. I heard that as a young man you were interested in Catholicism.

Eigen: When I was in my twenties. I think without quite verbalising it, I felt God in the flesh, that if there is spirit, it is embodied spirit. Catholicism seemed to give expression to a spirituality that encompassed spirit and flesh. But when I was taking instruction, exploring it, I got very sick and while I was sick, I recovered by reading novels, Saroyan and Faulkner, and that nursed me back to health. By the time I recovered I had the feeling that Catholicism was not my path. The priest giving instruction emphasised that Catholicism was a very rational religion. I wonder, might I have become Catholic if the priest had been more of a mystic? My body rejected it and I listened to my body.

Micha: And then you became interested in Buddhism?

Eigen: I've been interested in Buddhism and most religions I've come in contact with. I love religion, I have a real affinity for religions. I'm less doctrinaire than I was when I was young. I may be a Taoist now [laughs]. I like Taoism a lot. I like Hinduism and Buddhism. I go back and forth, each giving me something important.

I am a Jew. My father came from Austro Hungary. He wasn't religious here, nor was his father, nor my mother's parents. My mother's mother kept kosher and lit shabbos candles, and my mother kept kosher when I was a child so that her mother could come visit us. But my father was mainly interested in making a living. He came here as a teenager, and his father opened up a candy store for a time, but they came here as immigrants off the boat, and he deliberately did not learn English until he came here, because he didn't want to have an accent, and he didn't have an accent. He picked up an accounting book in a secondhand book store, learned accounting, and went up and down the streets asking stores if he could do their books, and he made enough money to go to law school and became a lawyer.

Micha: How did you start making the connection between psychoanalysis and mysticism?

Eigen: I took a psychology course when I was in college and it was terrible. It turned me off to psychology, but there were two paragraphs in the textbook that turned me on. One mentioned the unconscious and one talked about how the whole was greater than the sum of its parts—psychoanalysis and gestalt psychology. When I was in college, academic interest seemed mostly in mechanistic reflex psychology.

You asked me how I brought psychology and mysticism together. That is a hard question to answer, because I feel they were never really apart.

Micha: Well, I guess most people would see the disjunction in Freud's view of religion as a projection of our wishes or fears. And his belief that what is really real are the instinctive drives.

Eigen: Freud is very complicated. I've never heard him tell a lie. As a therapist, I can say that what he says is there. It may be slanted, it may be biased, it may be reductive, but paranoids see certain slivers of truth, and the kind of Nietzschean or Schopenhauerean truth that Freud sees is really so. He sees the will to power in sexual form, that we are driven, we are pressured, and we don't exactly know what to do with the whole thing.

Micha: Do you also see a different kind of subconscious, some kind of a super conscious, a layer of spiritual impulses that we are not aware of?

Eigen: I am not much of a theoretician. I don't start from the place where there is a distinction between the spirit and the rest of life. What we are dealing with is social–psycho–spiritual–physical. We can't say here is the spirit part, here is the emotional part, here is the intellectual part. If there were a model, it would be like a tapestry. Even with our brain structure, we can't say "Perception came first", or "memory came first", or "this came first". The parts of the brain work together, they compensate, they nourish each other, they conflict with each other, it's very alive, so you could say everything is spirit, everything is emotion, everything is mind, everything is body, whatever is your bias or your sensibility. All these things work together in a conspiratorial way all the time. Even antagonistic elements need each other.

Micha: But could you say that there are certain kinds of impulses or even abilities or connections that are usually hidden, and a normal consciousness that you could call the workaday consciousness . . .

Eigen: I see that as spiritual.

Micha: Ordinary consciousness is spiritual?

Eigen: Ordinary consciousness is tinged by spirit and formed by spirit. Whatever we do together affects our spirit. Someone could have a look that makes your spirit alive; someone else might have a look that throws a wet blanket on it. We transmit affective attitudes. This makes a difference to our day, to our growth, to how we feel about life, how life tastes to us. There is no transaction between people that does not have an affective quality or a spirit tonality that will affect you physically, mentally, spiritually, emotionally.

Micha: You don't want to create a hierarchy between spirit and other modes of being ...

Eigen: I'm not a big hierarchy person, because I find that if I have to be a hierarchy person, I would say that high is low and low is high. Once you start attending to something, realms and more realms keep opening up *ad infinitum*. No matter where you start, it opens up to everything else.

Micha: Is there such a thing as spiritual development, spiritual evolution? Can one move towards a higher realisation of who you are?

Eigen: I'm not that concerned with what is higher. It's hard enough trying to be a decent person here. I think our big job is to work with ourselves, on every level—socially, psychically, familially. It's not enough to be high in one way and beat your kids or scream at your kids or traumatise your kids on another plane. I've seen gurus and masters who are so high one way and are traumatising people right and left in another way. There is a certain sensitivity—you can call it spiritual if you like or emotional if you like—which is sensitivity to another person and to yourself with another person. How are you affecting that other person? That is the realm of spirituality I am most interested in.

Micha: I remember reading in your book, *Ecstasy* (2001), how you have found that people who are striving for a spiritual life, who have an active prayer life, who meditate are often what you call "ragers"—people who carry with them and release great reserves of anger.

Eigen: Yes, people may be meditators dedicated to the path, but get very impatient if something happens in real life that doesn't fit in with the calm and peace of the meditative state. I don't think that religious or spiritual people are immune to inflicting their personalities on others. This, for me, is the connection between psychoanalysis and spirituality. The issue is: how do we work with that? It's great to be in all kinds of spiritual states, but if you are in conflict with the guy next to you and you blow him away ... Nothing is more traumatising in personal relations than rage. I don't mind talking about spirituality, but any amount of spiritual realisation is worthless if you do that to someone else. I see embodying spiritual feeling more in terms of an evolution in sensitivity towards yourself and others. Religion is a tool to an extent, psychoanalysis is a tool to an extent, and there is no way to do it except to find within yourself what you are doing to other people, to feel the block, to feel the spark that becomes angry, the spark that becomes fearful, the spark that is pushed out on others, and to sit with it, pray with it, touch it, taste it.

Micha: On the collective level, when groups are pursuing some kind of intense religious agenda, do they also have the danger of flipping into some kind of violence or rage?

Eigen: Absolutely. I mean, if you have a violent God, and all religions have some kind of a violent God, then that's a project, a challenge. To the extent that God is a projection of our personality, and He says I'm going to get so angry if you don't do what I want, then that's not a very good model for raising your children (Eigen, 2002). You don't really have to do that with children. We don't have to do that with each other—beat each other up and go to war with each other. I think institutional injustices and familial injustices and personal injustices all have to be worked on together. You can't just work on institutional injustices without the actual people who are involved working on themselves, and you can't just work on yourself without working on the injustices in society.

Micha: How would you describe that connection between spiritual intensity and rage? Why is God angry, and why do people become angry?

Eigen: I think on an elemental level, we humans are a pretty violent group. It would be funny if the scientists are right and the universe began with an explosion, like a baby starts life with a scream. Then it's a scream that never stops, an explosion that never stops. And we are mediators of explosive capacity. One of the things that psychoanalysis has to offer is an awareness of how destructive we are. In a way, you might say, that psychoanalysis puts a barium tracer on our sense of destructiveness. The great psychoanalyst W. R. Bion has a formulation that is devastating. He talks about a force that goes on working after it has destroyed time, space, personality, and existence—a pure destructive force that never stops. Now I don't know if such a force exists . . .

Micha: Shiva [the Hindu god of destruction].

Eigen: Yes, exactly. There are intimations of it in all religions in some way. Freud talks about a destructive force against recovery. Melanie Klein talks about a destructive force within. Whatever names you want to give it, human destructiveness exists, whether it is left over from surviving in the wild, whether it is a predator–prey thing, a struggle for existence, or whether there is an inherent ecstasy in exercising one's power. We do destructive things. We're killers. We have killer psyches that we should feel guilty about. I think some of us have too little guilt, some of us have too much guilt, but we all have killer psyches, and we all injure each other and are injured. What do we do when we begin to realise that it is not just the other guys, that we all do it, and that we are in the middle of a sea of injury? We may also be in the middle of the sea of love, but we are also very dangerous and we do dangerous things to each other. The other guy is the bad guy, and I am the good guy. I am always the right one and you are always the wrong one, whether it is in a marriage, with kids, between groups, between nations. In my book, *Rage*, I note that an attitude that has perhaps done more harm in human history than any other is the sense of being right. Destruction goes on and on, except that some of us are catching on that it has been with us organising experience since the beginning. We are not going to get rid of it, but we can become more aware of how it works. We can—I wouldn't say transcend it, because that is going way too far—but we can make room for it, we can realise oh my God I am now about to bop this guy on the head because obviously he's wrong.

I recently saw the film *The Merchant of Venice*, with Al Pacino playing Shylock. Beautiful. You are brought up short, because you feel the gap between Shakespeare's days and ours, the gap and the immediacy. In those days, Shylock was supposed to be a comedian, a comic figure a joker . . . ha ha—look at the Jew with his stupid idea of justice as opposed to us beautiful, rich, privileged Christians who know mercy. When you see the film, the distance of four hundred years at once brings you up short and dissolves. The structure, for those who want to see it, involves beautiful people on the top paid for by abjection of those on the bottom, by the black slaves, by the denigration of the Jews, the slaughter of the Jews, the denigration of one kind of Jews by other kinds of Jews, this hierarchical denigration in which a group's ascendancy is always at the expense of someone else. That is a psychological, social, and spiritual problem.

Micha: And there is no way to become enlightened, to evolve, to be transformed? We can't get away from it?

Eigen: I think we can do something with it, but we have to sit with it, feel it, and taste it. We have to munch on it, we have to struggle with it, use our eyes, our ears, our taste buds. We have to say, "This doesn't taste good." Shylock was in the dirt and Christians laughed, "Ha, Ha", the victory of the good guys. But one needs to begin to feel that it doesn't taste good to see a human being in the dirt, just as it wouldn't taste good for oneself to be in the dirt. We are not dirt *now*, even if we say dust we were and dust we shall become. It is an evolutionary challenge to begin to develop sensitivity to see and experience this structure more deeply, how we put ourselves up at someone else's expense. Just sitting with this is something psychoanalysis does well. I think it very spiritual to dwell and work with our predicament. Psychoanalysis gives people time to sit with problems, taste tendencies, urges, needs, wishes, including what a shit one can be to others, and maybe you are a shit because your parents were shitty too, like their parents, or maybe it's just the way human beings are, because it is an explosive universe and we are explosive beings. And if you tell me my brain is programmed to be violent, well then screw my brain, maybe I can change my brain. Maybe I can alter my brain chemistry, a bit by will and intention, but also by weeping my heart out over who I am, who I'd like to be. Perhaps through psychotherapy and meditation and prayer brain chemistry can be altered, a shift made in better directions. I can say, "I don't like the make-up I've been given and don't have to fully give in to it. I don't have to fully give myself to it. I can resist, modulate, perhaps even change it."

Micha: And do you feel that help comes along from another dimension sometimes?

Eigen: I feel that what you call that other dimension is here, always here. Whatever you call God or spiritual reality is right here, in our lives. We are creating it and it is creating us through the way we are with each other, how we make each other feel. Do our interactions make a more kindly world or a less kindly world? It reminds me of what Judaism says—that my words are creating angels and devils.

Micha: Wherever it is coming from, you must see miracles in people's lives in therapy.

Eigen: I believe in miracles, I think we are miracles. I didn't ask for it, but when I was a young boy the sense of the holy came to me. It was animated by two incidents that I remember. One was by seeing the stars for the first time when I was two, and one was by seeing a particular rabbi, Rabbi Kellner, who came to the house to ask for donations. I looked forward to his visits because his face had a light that glowed, and I didn't know exactly what it was, but as I began to grow I realised it was a sense of the holy. That we are sacred, precious, that it is a precious gift to be alive, that we should try to do something deep with it. It's a sense that comes and goes, an animating sense of life. It doesn't take me outside of life. It brings me more fully into life. It brings more life, fuller life.

Micha: Have you met other people that you felt, like Rabbi Kellner, embodied, more than the usual, some kind of holiness?

Eigen: Well, almost, not quite, because I was young, that was my first hit. It's like your first love. But I'll tell you about a somewhat different but related kind of experience with three people—with Allen Ginsberg, D.W. Winnicott, and Rabbi Menachem Schneerson.

Micha: That's quite a combination of people. Can you tell me something about the experiences?

Eigen: The experience I had with Rabbi Schneerson and Allen Ginsberg and D.W. Winnicot was, I suppose, a bit mad, but a bit of madness sometimes opens doors.

Micha: You saw some kind of light coming from them . . .

Eigen: No. I thought they were me. This was a different experience than with Rabbi Kellner. I felt that they were me. When I met Allen Ginsberg for the first time, I looked at him and said, "He's me." I felt the same way when I met Winnicott. It wasn't like he could be me or I could be him, but "Oh my God, there I am." And I saw Rabbi Schneerson the same way. He was me. What I make of such experiences is that these people are feeding you your self, helping you access yourself, or a dimension of yourself. Someone else's being or face can somehow unconsciously give you support for who you are without necessarily saying a word, just by who *they* are.

Things like that happen in therapy with many variations. For instance, there are people who are in and out of hospitals, and deep down they are terribly self-hating people, feel bad about themselves, have extremely negative self-images which they may cover up. A major part of the therapy here is not interpreting the unconscious. The real work over the long haul is . . . what should we call it? So as not to be too "spiritual", let's call it affective transmission, emotional transmission. You are sitting there absorbing and seeing their vacuum or bad feelings that have been in their family, possibly for generations. Generations of bad feeling, generations of suffering. It's in the room, it's everywhere they go, like a cross, a black cloud, an agony that never lifts, a wound that never heals. You become that; you are that. You are making room for it, giving it a place to be. Some people unconsciously need to feel that someone feels how wounded they are, how awful they are. They don't want someone to say, you're really OK, it's not that bad. It *is* that bad. An ingredient needed is a deeply shared sense of how bad off one is, a state perhaps beyond words. But over the course of time, in the concentrated setting of therapy, that bad feeling meets, I don't know what to call it, a good feeling? A nicer feeling? However bad I am, some goodness gets transmitted, some good affect is transferred and builds. As time goes on, little by little, that bit of good affect, a kind of affect seed, begins to work on the bad feeling. The good can transmit while talking about deep trauma or simply about an interesting happening on the way to the office, or a good film, or the weather. A quiet emotional bell rings through varied communications and, over time, builds and works on the negativity. The person begins to feel a little safer, a little less catastrophic.

Micha: But with those three people you mentioned it just happened instantaneously?

Eigen: Yes, it just happened. With Allen Ginsberg, it was in North Beach, San Francisco. I was having a beer with some people, and this guy walked in and I said, "That's me!" I walked over to him and put my arms around him and he put his arms around me and we just looked at each other for a few seconds and then we parted. I saw him a number of times after that, and it never happened again.

Micha: What about W. R. Bion? You had a long-term relationship with Bion?

Eigen: No, that didn't happen with Bion, although Bion's words and presence carried special weight with me and changed my life (Eigen & Govrin, 2007). I taught and met Winnicott before Bion. I also met and taught Marion Milner and was the first to write about certain aspects of Winnicott and Milner. I met Winnicott in 1968 and Bion in 1977. Winnicott died in 1971 and Bion in 1979.

I gravitated towards Bion because he seemed to know more about destructive aspects of madness than anyone I ever read, except the poet William Blake. I began teaching Bion in order to learn from him and have been teaching Winnicott and Bion for over forty years. Bion gave seminars in New York City for a week in 1977, which I attended, and saw him for two therapy sessions. We talked about a lot of things, some out of the blue, some related to personal problems I raised. At one point he asked if I knew anything about Kabbalah, mentioning the *Zohar*. I said, "A little. I know it but don't *know* it." He was quick to say he knew it only a little, too. And then said, "I use the Kabbalah as a framework for psychoanalysis." I have not heard that he said that to anyone else. Some of my focus in writing about Bion has been on faith in relation to catastrophe, a basic Kabbalistic theme. One can find in Bion's descent into destructive aspects of madness a faith process, perhaps related implicitly to sparks of transformation and perhaps, even more deeply, no sparks at all, a null dimension, no dimension, in which everything has been nulled.

One finds through Bion deepening dialectics between faith and catastrophic aspects of personality, an eye on destruction and another on faith in the face of destruction, perhaps an impossible faith, a faith in the face of all destruction of faith that, nevertheless, is part of transformation. Aspects of Kabbalah emphasise sparks trapped in catastrophic realities in need of redemption, restoration. There is no place you can go where there are not hidden sparks in need of liberation. Wherever you find yourself, there is work to be done. Wherever you find yourself with a patient, you have to go.

There are certain patients whose truth is trauma, whose truth is that life is a lie, and that trauma happens. And you can't reassure them, you can't analyse it. They are stuck with some awful happening that they can't get past, that catastrophises their personality. With Bion fortifying me, so to speak, I am able to sit with people like that and not make a false move. Not say it's not there, not say it's not so bad. Something awful has happened, personality has been deformed and may be unalterable. It's not going to snap back into shape. You can only go further, you can't remake it.

Micha: What you are saying reminds me of something Reb Nachman of Bratzlav wrote, that the godless void created by the contraction of God's light is actually real on some level, and that there are certain *tzaddikim* who are able to look into that void—not to do anything, just to be able to look.

Eigen: That's exactly the case. There has been a massive alteration or deformation, and one experiences it and keeps on experiencing it. This would be my message to people in terms of helping the human race— help people experience their experience, not rush past it. Of course, you have to rush past it, you have to make a living, and so on. But there also has to be just sitting with what is. I wish Judaism did it a little better; I wish prayer did it a little better. Psychoanalysis is trying to make some contribution to it. I have a quote from a book of mine I want to read to you: "There are cases in which deep lines, cut by trauma, provide access to depths that are otherwise unreachable. In such instances, nourishment follows trauma to new places. We wish things could be otherwise, could be easier, but we have little choice when illumination shines through injury" (1999).
 I think that is a very Kabbalistic model.

Micha: Did you go on and study the *Zohar* or other Kabbalistic works?

Eigen: Well, a little. I'm a dabbler. I'm a spiritual dabbler in all these things. A number of spiritual threads are intertwined in my life and intertwined with therapy. Sometimes I think that I'm some kind of idiot savant, tuned into this one thing—a therapy moment, a therapy world in which psychic realities spread into many dimensions, many worlds. In therapy, one moment can be made of many worlds.

Micha: What do you think is going on in America today?

Eigen: I'll tell you one thing—and this is not just about America. I talk about madness a lot, but I don't think this is merely an age of madness. That would almost be a blessing. It is an age of psychopathy that makes use of madness. I think what we have more and more is psychopathic manipulation of psychotic anxieties—manipulation of dread of annihilation, apocalyptic fears. There are people who have a knack for being able to manipulate people's fears on a mass level. For example, about Iraq: "They have weapons of mass destruction." Or, more generally, implicitly: "If you don't listen to us you will be doomed." People are adept at using psychotic anxiety to get what they want. There are economic–political forces that can manipulate masses of people and, to a greater or lesser extent, control their minds by appealing to psychotic anxieties and structuring them in ways that will achieve what a certain political system wants. Who they are and what they want is grist for any good paranoid.

A wedding of economic elitism and religious fundamentalism is absolutely bloodcurdling. It justifies almost everything. These people have no doubt about what they are doing, no guilt about the injury they are causing other human beings. They're right, and they're powerful. And this is an important thing to think about for everyone—how self-righteousness obliterates guilt, and obliterates your feeling for other people. I've seen this not just with the power elite now, which is frightening. It's in the Bible. It's in the Quran. The psycho–social–spiritual challenge, basically, is that we have not finished evolving. I have a book called *The Sensitive Self* (2004), in which I call for an ethics of sensitivity, in which we sense each other as human beings. Shylock in *The Merchant of Venice* used to be a comic figure. At least today he is not a comic figure. It's a horror to see people treat one another that way. I think it's amazing that slavery exists, that it existed in this country so recently, that it was taken for granted in Shakespeare's times. It's mindboggling what we do to each other, but larger and larger parts of the population are saying we ought to live and let live, human beings are human beings. I saw the film *Hotel Rwanda*, where the Tutsis and the Hutu are killing each other. Large segments of the population do not want this to go on. But other segments vying for power keep on killing. We have a long way to go. Whether we will keep on evolving I don't know. Can we face our destructive power or the high that power gives us, a self-intoxication that wipes out guilt and sensitivity? A book I wrote recently, *Age of Psychopathy*, adds more details to the present challenge and can be downloaded: http://tinyurl.com/yal4wth.

Micha: A lot of people are on a spiritual search, in Israel as well as elsewhere. What should people be aware of when looking for a guru, so that they shouldn't get involved with someone who is manipulative and will hurt them in the final analysis?

Eigen: Well, all human beings are manipulative to a certain extent. I don't know what to do with gurus. I worked with several gurus. One was Swami Muktananda in the 1960s. He represented himself as facing all the demons of the unconscious and transcending erotic enticements, an impossible goal for me, one that persecuted me for many years. Later, I learnt that he was sleeping with those he was helping. There is no guru who is not a human being. There is no guru who is all that different from you. I got a lot from Chogyam Trungpa, who also was sleeping with his charges, some of whom were badly injured. He made no secret of it. One of my friends went on a solitary mountain retreat for two weeks under Chogyam's guidance and when he returned said to his teacher, "I'm a different man. When I look at women now, I no longer see them with the same hungry desire but as persons like myself." "Look again!" Chogyam said.

The kind of intimacy and opening touched in these relationships raises the emotional–spiritual stakes. One can well sympathise with Odysseus needing to be tied to the deck in order to withstand the sirens' song. But, in certain circumstances, even that might not do the trick. Not only gurus, but psychotherapists are not immune to currents that arise when two are close.

The experience I had with Rabbi Schneerson or Allen Ginsberg or D. W. Winnicott brings us close to an important issue. What are they supporting in you? What are they helping more fully into life? What kind of birth process is being mediated (Eigen, 2014b)? In assimilating the "You are me" experience, I had the feeling that I was being given to myself in some important way. We are here to support each other into fuller life and to help do this with ourselves as well. In the end, it is you whom you are going to be living with twenty-four hours a day for the rest of your life, and not with a guru or anyone else. Being with a guru is not going to save you from your job, which is to feel what it feels like to be you. And this also involves feeling the impact that this man or woman is having on you. Nobody likes any guru one hundred per cent for everything. The Dalai Lama is narrow-minded in some ways. He doesn't understand a lot of things. I'm not sure he has reached the self-hate and self-destruction of some patients I have described to you today. I suspect this kind of self-hate is somewhat foreign to him and not something he grew up with as first or second nature.

Being with the Dalai Lama can give you a lot, perhaps something crucial. But you also have to feel, "What part of me is being left out?" You can apply what I am saying in many therapy situations, not just meditation communities. No one has everything for you and no one can save you from the work you have to do with yourself. You have to find your own way of being with yourself, working with yourself. Something I've never liked about the mental health field is how they pathologise so many idiosyncratic things about people. There is no one way to be healthy. Your way is not going to be the same as the Dalai Lama's or Rabbi Schneerson's. But perhaps they can help set you free to some extent, so that you can find your own way of being healthy. It doesn't mean that you are not going to be warped, or that you won't have this problem or that problem. You'll just have a better way of being a problematic being. It won't be your spouse's way, your children's way. It will be the particular touch, the particular taste you bring to life.

CHAPTER NINE

Jumping in*

Jan Niemira (JN): Should we just jump in?

Michael Eigen (ME): Yes.

JN: What do you recall as most valuable about your training experience? Do you remember learning something that struck you as particularly important? Did anything strike you as unimportant? And is there anything you've had to unlearn?

ME: I had a lot of supervision and control work, yet the most important thing was being left alone to do what came out of me with patients. When I wasn't interfered with too much, I could learn how to be with people.

I should make special mention of New Hope Guild, a private clinic in Brooklyn, New York, where I worked for many years. Not only did it give me a chance to become myself, but I met my wife there! Every week the head of the clinic, Sherman Schachter, had clinical meetings

---

* An interview that accompanied Jan Niemira's book review of *Flames From the Unconscious: Trauma, Madness and Faith in Psychoanalytic Perspectives*, 2011.

with the staff. These weekly meetings on clinical issues were important for many reasons. It gave us all a chance to hear something about what other therapists were doing and exchange feedback in an open atmosphere. I learnt a lot about complexities of dependence. The atmosphere was one of being devoted to the patient, supporting the therapist–patient relationship. There were plenty of patients waiting to be seen with all kinds of problems: masochism, acting out, anxiety, depression, paranoia, and what they called chronic schizophrenia. Character disorder was a popular category. This usually meant people so wounded and damaged they would need help possibly all life long: deep, supportive help, a kind of help, so to speak, deeper than analysis.

New Hope Guild had an analytic atmosphere that was deeply supportive of the patient–therapist dyad. Support the work; support the atmospheric conditions. I went through the training programme, taught, supervised. Some therapists who became well known passed through my seminars or supervision at the time. Jessica Benjamin took my Winnicott seminar, one of the first to be given in the city. Muriel Dimen was in supervision with me for a while. My seminars were an early burst of the British school in New York. My paper on working with "unwanted" patients summarised some of my work here (Eigen, 1993).

It was a time when you could take time. It seems the economic press is greater today. It is harder to feel unrushed. Today, much more time is spent with reports and fulfilling administrative do's and don'ts. In those days I was able to feel OK making little money and in training, you don't make much money—it's a kind of slave status or, to dignify that, apprenticeship status. I felt I was immersed in a kind of timeless apprenticeship, where the work I loved had a chance to grow in its own way. You steeped. You brewed. You let the psyche grow. You grow into yourself. You had time for psyche, psyche-time, time to be there person-to-person, psyche-to-psyche, without wondering who's looking over your shoulder. And whenever I got into trouble with patients—and I did get into trouble, I was kind of maniacal at times, especially with kids—Sherman always came through with some sublime remark that took the air out of the situation.

JN: Do you remember a particular one?

ME: One thing I came to on my own was discovering that I was at risk for injury while working with kids. I would overextend myself. I would want to be the therapeutic agent, or the substitute parent, or the provider of the good in this awful world. And so if a kid said, "Let's climb up on the roof of the garage," we'd climb up a tree and go on the roof of the garage and dance around and do crazy things. Over time, I realised I was getting injured in sessions. I mean minor physical injuries, falls, cuts, bruises. I'd get hurt by a game we were playing. I began to get a sense that there was a little man inside, a little signal that I began to realise I wasn't listening to. And the signal system would say something like, if I can translate it into words: "Don't. No. This is going to be too much. This is off. This is too far. Draw back." And I began to think, well, am I a psychic sissy? A psychic wimp? I'm going to draw back and not go all the way? And then I thought about basketball players and how you say about a good basketball player, he plays within himself, within his limits, he plays his own game. So, I had to begin to find my own game, so to speak, and not be swept up with the other person's enthusiasm; learn to hold a little of myself back so there would be more room for the both of us.

When I began therapy with adults, I thought all I had to do was be like my therapist and my patients would be like me. I would be my therapist, do what he does. And then I began to realise, "Oh, my God! The patients I'm seeing *aren't* like me. There are different kinds of people, different breeds with different needs. What works with me isn't necessarily going to work with them." I had to go through the awful separation of realising I couldn't simply be my therapist with my patients; I'd have to find a way of being with this particular person, this set of needs, this unique safe combination. Do we have a safe inside where we lock our valuables? My psyche had to get to work and break with, separate from, my therapist when it came to working with people in the trenches. One needs more than formulae and identifications to begin to find what nutriments, what set of responses would actually work in this situation.

JN: I want to ask you a question about the book *Flames from the Unconscious* (2009). In Chapter Five, "I killed Socrates", you discuss what you call a "spreading I". The last paragraph of this section reads, "there is a psycho or mad dimension to thinking–feeling that is there at all times. And one way it works is *spreading boundlessness, boundlessspread*. Deniers are not free of boundless spread. They smear others with the denied element or some substitution for it. One paints the world with feelings in semi-blind ways". Wow. Can you elaborate on what you mean by a "spreading I"? On what you mean by "spread"?

ME: It's a theme, an issue, an experience, sets of experiences that have concerned me ever since I can remember thinking about these things. Even before therapy. How permeable we are. Walt Whitman says, "I am multitudes". Rimbaud says, "I am an other". We don't really know what we're talking about when we talk about I-feeling or self-feeling or identity-feeling, me-feeling, but it's there, and it drives us. Freud's identificatory I can attach to anything. It can idealise. It can denigrate. It can idealise faeces or a flag. It can denigrate sublime and beautiful things. It works in many gradations and polarities. If you begin to live your way into it more, you may find some kind of identification going on all the time with everything.

One thing I got something out of was the exposure I had with Fritz Perls. He might suggest that a person begin telling a dream by saying, "This dream is my existence". Then, he might pick parts of the dream and suggest the dreamer become that part. One would become a table corner, a sunbeam ray, a baby . . . There's no limit to our identificatory capacity.

At the same time that we are connected, or in union, with everything, we're also distinct. This balance of identification and distinction is what I call the distinction–union structure because both elements are always co-present and nourish and antagonise each other (Eigen, 2011b). A kind of DNA and RNA of the psyche. Each psychic act is characterised by this double tendency. And this double tendency is a unity, a system. We have all kinds of aberrations of the system, disjunctions of distinction–union, denial of one or the other. "I'm afraid of being distinct." "I'm afraid of uniting."

Films play this out, dividing various degrees of distinction–union among characters. Often there is a more "union" type of person or a more "separate" type of person, and you see some kind of reversal, so that each discovers his/her other side by the film's end. Films portray dramas between tendencies. Some kind of fusion or merger is going on at the same time as some withholding, some distinction. Combinations and intensities shift at various speeds. This doubleness–oneness applies to many dimensions, for example, presence–absence. One moment I'm here but not here, I'm not really as in it as I seem. Another moment I'm more in it than I seem. Union, detachment, presence, absence . . . each can be explosive, work in varied ways.

The detachment aspect seems to be less explosive, but that depends on how it is programmed. Detachment can calculate strategies for explosive action. The affective background of detachment plays a role in how detachment is used. Detachment can express hidden contempt, looking down at the world, take the air out of life. It can have contempt for the impulsive or affiliative side. "You have to be a dummy to have an affiliative side. But me? My detached observing ego won't get taken in by anything." It's how these capacities are used that matters. You can value the separation side, you can value the union side, but we need to develop both. We have to learn how to use capacities that constitute us. We didn't make up this double capacity, we didn't create it. We find it organising our lives. We find that it's part of our equipment, and one of our great challenges is what to do with it, how to partner capacities that are part of our make-up.

JN: On page 102, in a very poignant account of her experience of herself, the other (her therapist), and their being together, Grace says, "There are void people and there are fullness people. That we're together proves that different souls work together, *must* work together. I release you into your fullness, and you release me into my void." This brought tears to my eyes. But it also sounds like a statement about genetic allotments of some kind. Different types of instincts, maybe, or pre-primitive psychic substances and anti-substances? Maybe it points to soul or karma? Could you share your thoughts on fullness people and void people?

ME: How we become constituted as more this or that exercises Freud. For Freud, it was how instincts were organised, and this had developmental, environmental, and genetic components, but he was not willing to put more on genetics than he had to in terms of life's traumas leading to ways basic capacities become organised.

At the end of *The Electrified Tightrope*, the afterword, I talked about therapists who are more adult or more child-like, and patients who are more child patients or adult patients, and how often they can become mismatched. You have a child therapist with an adult patient, or a child patient with an adult therapist, or other combinations. My feeling is that certain people are destined to be more child-like all their lives. I suspect I'm one of them. It's good for such a person, then, to become a better child, a fuller child, rather than try to become a make-believe adult that he can't be. So if I have an adult therapist who's trying to make me more like him, so to speak, he may be trying to evolve me into the wrong kind of person. He may not appreciate my child-like, playful nature. Perhaps the job would be to help me become a better playmate, a fuller playmate, a richer playmate: relate to the playground in a way that works better, is less destructive, works better for everybody. And, likewise, I have to realise, as a child therapist, that I may have an adult patient and have to refer him to an adult therapist or, if we work together, respect the difference and sense that we are developing along different developmental tracks. Not that he lacks a child, but he has an adult organisation that has to be free to develop along its own line.

Something of this principle, I suspect, applies to more full or void people. I think that the two tendencies, or organisations, plentitude and void, the cup runneth over and the empty cup, are crucial moments of existence. We need to live our way into both, make room for both, be less scared of either side. Fullness can be scary because of the intensity. It's too much. Void can be terrifying because you're afraid you're going to disappear, there'll be nothing, and you haven't discovered how freeing no-thing can be. There's a dialectical, or, in Winnicott's terms, a paradoxical, relationship between these capacities, and a void person will have to develop the fullness aspect in her/his own way and the fullness person will have to develop the void aspect in her/his own way. At the same time, it says in the *Talmud*, go from strength to strength. Don't play down your strength. If your strength is in the fullness area, then your job is to mine it. To work the field, farm it. Your job is to do something with what you are given. If your strength is in the void area, your job is to cultivate it. Bring it out. Let it evolve, develop, and open up to the realities that it opens for you.

JN: At times, *Flames from the Unconscious* is very optimistic and points to joyful, transcendent states alongside some very, very dark ones. In fact, the final words of the book are "Joy is joyful". Do you think of yourself generally as an optimist? Joyful?

At other times, there is a pessimistic tone, less hopeful about the possibility of transforming or finding a safe place for a destructive pulse, but rather a lament looking back at how we've failed to do so. You say, "The boundless supporting other has been wounded and repair is not in sight. Deformations of the self and society spiral"

(p. 26). Then, later, I noticed what might be a typo or might be what you intended to say, but I wondered if it were a slip. Regarding the "bully government" of very recent years, you say, "A kind of psychopathic element rules the day. But it is not the only element. It is now the only path we can take. So many of us want something better, fuller, more caring than this. A caring for conditions that support life" (p. 142). Did you mean "It is *now* the only path we can take?"

ME: No, I didn't. You definitely picked up on a typo. It's *not* the only path we can take. We have many sub-currents. We have a psychopathic element, that's for sure. Everyone's psychopathic today, whoever they are. I don't care what they present themselves as, it's endemic. It's in the world atmosphere. But that's not our only current. That's not our only possibility.

I won't go back to the year 2000 and the election the Bush group stole. The way the Supreme Court perjured itself set an example. If the highest court in the land perverts itself, you'd be a dummy not to do whatever you felt would be to your advantage. Along with this is the mushrooming of the financial industry, deregulation, the spiralling of thinking processes connected with new ways to make money. The mathematical mind applied to financial manipulation. And since we have a kind of genius mind that doesn't quite know what to do with itself, it keeps finding new pathways to be creative in. It shot the rocket ship into outer space with financial creativeness and nearly brought the system down.

There's immense psychopathy on all levels (Eigen, 2006b). There's a big push in psychoanalysis to be more psychopathic. I'm not saying Freud wasn't psychopathic, he sure was, so was Jung, but that's not all they were. They had a creative psychopathy, an exploratory psychopathy as well. It wasn't only psychopathic. But we are pushed more and more toward psychopathic elements in practice. Like lying to get insurance. People put down a diagnosis they think is going to work on an insurance claim. The whole insurance game is so perverse anyway and the meaning of diagnosis is so . . . it's almost a perversion of the personal to have to capsulise a person in diagnostic terms in a way that will fit a system. A psychopathic element creeps into psychoanalysis because of the rule of economic needs.

But there are other sub-currents. In the UN, for example, there are both nasty and helpful tendencies, genuine attempts to work with world health and food problems. There's a wish to help: a wish to help others and a wish to be helped in a real way. There's a genuine caring that is in competition with the psychopathic element. In a way, this is both an Age of Psychopathy and an Age of Sensitivity. The dominant tendency at the moment seems to be economic psychopathy, but it is not the only current.

I think of a good man who ran for mayor in New York and lost, and, when asked about his feelings about the loss, said something like, "I cut my nerve endings a long time ago. You can't have sensitive nerves and be in politics." If people who run the show denigrate and reject personal pain, they're going to cause pain and not feel it or care about its consequences. If there's one thought that needs to be respected in the social system in the world today, it's that helping people is OK. Yet, there are strong currents against this attitude.

Winnicott, more than any worker I knew, developed a tone and style and body of work in which there was no shame attached to being dependent. A primary biblical message that Jesus ratified: "Help the needy, the poor". It's an attitude that goes a long way, applies to many spheres of experience.

There's no shame in dependency. In Jung, there's shame for being dependent, for example, lightly veiled contempt for weakness in contrast with his own ability to pull himself up. In Freud, there's a push away from dependency, and, in most developmental theories that I grew up with, Mahler for one, there was a push toward individuation. In Klein's work, too, you get a sense if you're paranoid–schizoid, you're bad, if you're depressive, you're better, a kind of psychoanalytic moralism, superiority of "advanced" over "primitive" positions. In Winnicott, there was more back and forth, more of a balance, less judgemental tolerance of dependent elements, even the possibility of creative dependency. I think this is one of the things I instinctively picked up at New Hope Guild. Sherman, in one of our meetings, said that when we're talking about our patients, we're often talking about dependency. For many, lifelong dependency because the damage is so great that lifelong support may be needed. Winnicott tends not to shame such needs.

A clinical atmosphere that didn't make one feel bad for who one is. It helped me with my own lifelong dependency. To work with who you are without condemnation is an attitude that needs to be assimilated by the larger culture as well as oneself. It hasn't been, except in small, constricted ways. A recent president of my country said, "Feelings are for sissies." In response to this kind of attitude, I wrote a book called *Feeling Matters*, and before that, *The Sensitive Self*, in which, in my own tiny, drop-in-the-ocean fashion, I tried to valorise the importance of our feeling life, our feeling world. This little substream has to play a larger role in the social body. Prophets have been saying so for a long, long time.

JN: You mention Prometheus, Socrates, and the serpent in the Garden of Eden in this book. All of these figures brought illumination to mankind against the will of powerful others. It didn't end well for any of them. Do you feel as though you might be saying something unpopular in this book?

ME: Popular and unpopular. Definitely unpopular, but popular to a certain soul-thread. It's an old narrative. It's an ancient narrative coming out in psychoanalytic ways. A kind of recycling, but not just recycling, because psychoanalysis adds new ground. For example, it was the "area of faith" paper I wrote that turned out to be the first in psychoanalysis that talked about Winnicott's use of the object (Eigen, 1981, 1993). I felt Winnicott's "use of object" formulation was an evolution of psychic reality. It constituted a leap in psychic experiencing. Just like Rilke's poems create psychic reality as he writes, this opened a door. So, I don't think psychoanalysis is *just* recycling an ancient narrative. There are overlaps with biblical, Hindu, Buddhist concerns. Freud remarked to Fliess that they were very much in the tradition of ancient mystery cults, concerned with transformation. Linked with ancient wisdom but creating variations, further paths, and ways of framing evolutionary challenges.

One part of the human condition is that our products are ahead of our ability to assimilate them. We produce thoughts, we produce products, and we produce technological knowhow way ahead of our ability to assimilate them. We produce experiences, but our capacity to digest them is far behind. So, I think that we haven't digested what psychoanalysis is producing. An assimilation process hasn't caught up with pathways that are opening.

JN: I know we're approaching our time, but I have one more question. There are some instances in the book where you explicitly reference a verbal *exchange* between you and someone you're working with. I'm thinking of the scene where Sea sees you eating, destroying a pear, and another when discussing a patient's desire for "interpenetrating harmonious mix-up". These exchanges sound like profound experiences in the consulting room. Yet, while about half of the book is associative material, both yours and others', the dialogue seems to be between psy*ches* that are seemingly as alone together as possible. Can you say more about what this looks like in the consulting room? How does this translate into technique? How and when do you intervene or interpret?

ME: So many elements play into it. It could be that I'm hungry or impulsive, or I just wanted to eat the pear and I wasn't thinking of my patient whatsoever, and the patient notices and begins talking about my pear-eating activity, and then I begin meditating that we're all killers. That we kill to eat. Even plants. There's no way to avoid our predatory nature. And she takes off on her associative path to the murders, the soul murders, the psychic murders of her past. And it turns out to be fruitful that we're sort of playing on each other's dreads. It might be that this is a defect in technique on my part or a defect in my person, that I should eat a pear in a session and not take care of my needs outside the session.

Patients have to put up with me, make a lot of allowances. It could be part of narcissism to say that's part of growth processes, that we have to make allowances for each other. We have to cut each other slack in order to be with each other at all. But that's true in relationships, any relationship. If you can't cut each other slack, you're not going to be able to tolerate being with each other in a growth-producing way. In this particular instance, psyche fed psyche, so to speak. The feeding situation turned into a fruitful psychic event.

JN: Another one was a situation where a patient learnt that you were ill and had wanted to have sex with you, seeking what you put in quotes as an "interpenetrating harmonious mix-up".

ME: That was in the first or second chapter. I was writing on Winnicott's aloneness. Winnicott writes about a certain primordial aloneness, an aloneness that runs through life, and the importance for Winnicott of having this aloneness supported in infancy. In another chapter, in another book, *Contact with the Depths* (2011b), there's an application of Winnicott's finding, a deep finding, the fact that aloneness has to be supported. How can aloneness be supported? The best kind of support, Winnicott seems to feel, is that it is supported by support one doesn't even know one has. A kind of seamless support, which I call support by the boundless, infinite unknown. There's a chapter in *Contact with the Depths* in which I show that in addiction there is wounded aloneness seeking repair or communication. In therapy, you become a kind of background support for wounded aloneness to evolve. There are so many ins and outs of therapeutic work. You have to be Kernberg and Kohut at the same time, and so much more.

The sessions I had with Bion took many forms in a short time. He remarked that if I were seeing him on a regular basis he might not do as much, but since we were only meeting these few times, he spoke a lot. Out of the blue, he brought up the Kabbalah. I'm thinking of Kabbalah now with you because of the upcoming Kabbalah meeting I'll be doing. I'm doing a series of psychoanalysis and Kabbalah meetings for the New York University Postdoctoral Contemplative Studies Project (Eigen, 2012a, 2014a,b). Out of the blue, he looks at me and says, "Do you know the Kabbalah? The *Zohar*?" I said, "Well, I know the *Zohar*, but I don't *know* the *Zohar* . . ."

He says, "Neither do I." He pauses, then says, "I use Kabbalah as a framework for psychoanalysis." We talked about that a while. Then, at another point in the session, he looks at me and says, "You know, you ought to get married." He says, "Marriage isn't what you think it is. It's a relationship between two people speaking truth to each other, that mitigates the severity to yourself."

JN: Wow.

ME: I got married four years later. At first I wondered, does he say the same thing to everybody? I checked with one of my girlfriends who saw him and the answer is a definitive no. He told her, "You're not ready for marriage. You have an unworked out father problem." [Eigen laughing.] So, where do these things come from? Oracular pronouncements out of the blue that clinically, technically, seem to be inappropriate. One shouldn't and wouldn't say such things within a certain moral code, but it would be immoral not to if one's psychic connection is accurate and true and helpful and caring and compassionate. And these were compassionate remarks. He was making contact with something, psyche to psyche. I think of a text in which he says the job of the therapist is to introduce the patient to him/herself. He was introducing me to aspects of myself that I may have dissociated, or put down, or devalued. It was very helpful, very freeing and challenging.

Someone could say this is wild analysis. Isn't this wild analysis? Well, wouldn't it be impoverished if there weren't some wild analysis? Maybe we have to cultivate wild analysis so it won't be destructive, so it can be creative and constructive, the constructive aspect of wild analysis, because it's more destructive not to have that element when it's pertinent.

JN: I think we're at the end of our hour.

ME: What was the other question? You had one more.

JN: It was a question about Dr Z. Dr Z says, "And psychotherapy. How can it help? Offer compensation for not being able to do anything? To contact oneself? To taste differently, to touch a few others who come one's way, to open wombs, other doors?" I love this sentence because it captures such an intense moment. Later, you say, "A lot of therapy is about the slow recovery of faith" (p. 136). Given the political horrors you reference throughout the book, can you say more about how you think therapy or analysis can help? Is this something that can be taught?

ME: Let me just hit a thread. Where did I get "Z" from? Winnicott talks about X time that mother's away from baby, mother comes back, baby recovers. X plus Y time away from baby, mother comes back, baby a little more shaky but comes back OK enough. X plus Y plus Z time away from the baby, and there's a permanent alteration to the psyche. Yes, the baby comes back, but in what form? Altered. Something else. Maybe a deformity's been added. Sometimes we get reborn as monsters, sometimes we get reborn as shrunken, sometimes we get reborn as rageful, but something happens to us and we're not the same. How could we be the same?

My wife and I were once on a desert tour with a guide. He pointed to a cactus and spoke of how the cactus grows. He said the branches of the cactus grow out from places the cactus has been wounded. Branches grow from the cactus's wounds. The 'Z' dimension is a place where we underwent permanent alteration in Winnicott's terms. Freud talked about permanent alteration of the psyche in "Analysis terminable and interminable". Permanent alterations of the psyche at certain points. I write about this in *Psychic Deadness* (1996) in detail. What I'm now calling the Z dimension is that dimension where there's permanent alteration. Balint (1968) talked about regressions that could be worked with and malignant regressions that can't be worked with. The latter is the Z dimension. We have in psychoanalysis subsections of the field working with the Z dimension. We did that in being able to work with borderlines. Borderlines have stimulated growth of response systems to meet the Z dimension, to a certain extent. We've done that with psychosis. If someone comes into our office, like Schreber, and talks about soul murder, we know immediately, empathically, something about soul murder and begin to find out how his soul was murdered (Eigen, 1986). It's not a foreign concept. We enter the Z dimension with this psychotic patient. We have *not* learnt how to do that with psychopaths and we have to. Because this is *the* problem of our age. If we can't work with psychopaths, the human enterprise will go down the tubes. We have to learn how to work with the Z dimension of our psychopathic tendency and that is upfront in evolution even if it takes two thousand years.

A post-interview note

Our psychopathic tendency has given us a lot. It helped us survive. But it mainly or only cares about staying alive and does not care how it manages to do this. Anything goes in the service of the self getting what it thinks it wants or needs. I have spoken about madness in the service of psychopathy, but there are ways our psychopathic tendency itself becomes deranged.

The constellation of things has changed, is changing. How we survive, with what quality, is increasingly important. We endanger life, the earth, the atmosphere, and our own spirit with toxins that are part of survival at any cost. Survival at any cost on a grand scale can become very destructive to survival, as well as affecting the microstructures of our souls. A tall learning process is in order and we do not know what it is we need to learn. One formulation: how to nourish what is productive in our psychopathic tendency, its creative life-giving aspect, while limiting a hypertrophic momentum that maims existence.

There comes a point where the cost of survival is more than we can bear. The very taste and feel of existence becomes poisoned by the ways we survive. At some point, something more is needed and faith that there is something more begins to play a role in how we survive. Issues of quality and worth press for a hearing. It is through the organ of faith that we hear the heartbeat of existence. But even faith can be poisoned and poisonous, in need of repair. How do we taste to ourselves and others? When we listen, what do we hear?

CHAPTER TEN

Future as unknown presence (even if it is absent)

What is the future? It engulfs me, attracts me. I plunge into it, swim in it. How is it different from past or present? A time monster with three heads and who knows how many feet and hands? A Hindu saying: Dream life is the present, waking life the past, dreamless sleep (void) the future.

Time so often feels timeless. Sessions sometimes drag by. Time could not go slower. Even slowness is timeless. Or they speed by. High velocity timelessness. Too fast, too slow, just right. The Goldilocks of time.

There is a sense of dropping down into oneself. Silent. Deep into invisible soil, dropping ... A kind of blackout. Schreber described a kind of blackout in which world and self ceased, then reappeared in a new key, "miracled up".

To sink and sink into the future, uncreated futures of a session, uncreated time. Time as creation, future as creative moments that nourish, terrify, uplift, challenge, soften, baffle. Future as approaching womb.

Bion writes, "The real nature of psychoanalytic methodology has never been properly assessed". He has psychoanalytic intuition in mind, which seems to span time, making use of past, present, future, timelessness.

Where does one go when one sinks through the bottoms of sessions?

Where is one waiting?

An idea, a feeling, an image form. Time is back. You look at the clock. There is still forty minutes to go. You are both still there. Where did the bottom of the session go? Now that you are back, you appreciate bottomless more. Maybe if you are quiet and still enough, you can sink again and go through. Maybe if you are quiet enough, the session will find you.

Do you ever feel you are being created by the future of the session? Something without bottom or sides or top? The session is creating you?

Psychoanalytic time—how to nurture it so that it nurtures you.

The patient is everywhere. The patient is a point, now seeable, now vanishing.

You hear a cry and feel it all through life. A soundless cry that creates existence. Or, as the psalm says, "I go to bed weeping and wake up laughing". A presence bottomless beyond touch touches you.

AFTERWORD

Faith-work

The psyche can only take so much of itself. Only so much build-up of emotion, pressure, and tension is tolerable.

Freud spoke of flooding as a primal trauma. Flooded by intensity, emotion, stimulation, nothingness. What our nature produces can be ahead of its capacity to process and digest. We are traumatised by incapacity to tolerate and work with what happens to us and within us. Traumatised by our own emotional reality.

Not all life is catastrophic. There is much joy, pleasure, beauty, bliss, goodness. Yet, catastrophe is a thread that runs through it, sometimes more, less. Psychoanalysis notes that the very push and pressure of being an emotional being has catastrophic aspects and consequences.

Psychoanalysis sets a task: if we do not find ways of meeting fears that haunt and beset us, we are in danger. We are in danger anyway, tossed, as Taoist sages say, like rag dolls by waves of emotional intensities with little capacity to sustain them. Paradoxical beings challenged to develop capacities to work with a baffling nature. We have "successful" moments, but it cannot be said that we know what we are doing. Perhaps we ask ourselves to do what we cannot do. If that is so, it is a situation worth acknowledging and letting in. If we keep the great unknown in the foreground, perhaps we can learn more about what we *can* do with less belligerence.

Some scholars see the Kabbalah as a response to catastrophe. It touches dimensions in which faith, mystical experience, and catastrophe are linked. The link between faith and catastrophe takes many forms.

What can faith do in situations with no solution, no way out? It is one of the mysteries of faith that, at times, it helps us sit with, suffer and grow through such situations. A striking expression of such a moment is the biblical Job's, "Yay, though You slay me yet will I trust You". A person in a group I taught described this as "an ultimate moment".

Another is Jesus saying, "Father, why have you forsaken me?" In the face of death, faith. In the face of loss of faith, faith.

Faith is a vehicle that radically opens experiencing and plays a role in building tolerance for experience. This is what faith faces, must face. It is germane to the fervour and possibility of existence, tension, and struggle, with roots in grace. Faith rooted in profound grace, deeper than catastrophe, a sense that has an impact on the flavour of our lives.

So many sessions are crises of faith, whether precipitated by hate or love. Crises in the face of violence done to the soul from within and without: real, but also imaginal in terrifying magnification.

My soul calls to you from the depths, cries the psalms. A part of the heart joy, a part of the heart sorrow, dread, rage. Soul beyond hearing, touching, indefinable presence touching you.

REFERENCES

Balint, M. (1968). *The Basic Fault*. London: Tavistock.
Barfield, O. (1984). *Poetic Diction: A Study in Meaning*. Middletown, CT: Wesleyan University Press.
Bion, W. R. (1965). *Transformations*. London: Karnac, 1984.
Bion, W. R. (1970). *Attention and Interpretation*. London: Karnac, 1984.
Bion, W. R. (1977). Youtube Video of Bion in Tavistock. www.youtube.com/watch?v=3GDbHdycKCY
Bion, W. R. (1980). *Bion in New York and Sao Paulo*. Strathtay, Perthshire: Clunie Press.
Bion, W. R. (1982). *The Long Week-End 1887–1919: Part of a Life*. London: Karnac.
Bion, W. R. (1994). *Cogitations*, F. Bion (Ed.). London: Karnac.
Bion, W. R. (2001). *A Memoir of the Future*. London: Karnac, 2004.
Bohm, D. (1980). *Wholeness and the Implicate Order*. London: Routledge, 2002.
Eddington, A. S. (1928). *The Nature of the Physical World*. London: Macmillan.
Eigen, M. (1973). Abstinence and the schizoid ego. *International Journal of Psychoanalysis*, 54: 493–498. Reprinted in: A. Phillips (Ed.), *The Electrified Tightrope* (pp. 1–8). London: Karnac, 1993.

Eigen, M. (1977). On working with 'unwanted' patients. *International Journal of Psychoanalysis, 58*: 109–121.
Eigen, M. (1981a). The area of faith in Winnicott, Lacan and Bion. *International Journal of Psychoanalysis, 62*: 413–433. Reprinted in: A. Phillips (Ed.), *The Electrified Tightrope* (pp. 109–138). London: Karnac, 1993.
Eigen, M. (1981b). Guntrip's analysis with Winnicott—a critique of Glatzer and Evans. *Contemporary Psychoanalysis, 17*: 103–111. Reprinted in: A. Phillips (Ed.), *The Electrified Tightrope* (pp. 139–146). London: Karnac, 1993.
Eigen, M. (1986). *The Psychotic Core*. London: Karnac, 2004.
Eigen, M. (1992). *Coming Through the Whirlwind*. Wilmette, IL: Chiron.
Eigen, M. (1993). *The Electrified Tightrope*, A. Phillips (Ed.). London: Karnac Books, 2004.
Eigen, M. (1995). *Reshaping the Self: Reflections on Renewal in Therapy*. London: Karnac, 2013.
Eigen, M. (1996). *Psychic Deadness*. London: Karnac, 2004.
Eigen, M. (1998). *The Psychoanalytic Mystic*. London: Free Association Books.
Eigen, M. (1999). *Toxic Nourishment*. London: Karnac.
Eigen, M. (2001). *Ecstasy*. Middletown, CT: Wesleyan University Press.
Eigen, M. (2002). *Rage*. Middletown, CT: Wesleyan University Press.
Eigen, M. (2004). *The Sensitive Self*. Middletown, CT: Wesleyan University Press.
Eigen, M. (2005). *Emotional Storm*. Middletown, CT: Wesleyan University Press.
Eigen, M. (2006a). *Feeling Matters*. London: Karnac.
Eigen, M. (2006b). *Age of Psychopathy*. www.psychoanalysis-and-therapy.com/human_nature/eigen/pref.html.
Eigen, M. (2009). *Flames from the Unconscious: Trauma, Madness, and Faith*. London: Karnac.
Eigen, M. (2010). *Eigen in Seoul Vol. 1: Madness and Murder*. London: Karnac.
Eigen, M. (2011a). *Eigen in Seoul Vol. 2: Faith and Transformation*. London: Karnac.
Eigen, M. (2011b). *Contact with the Depths*. London: Karnac.
Eigen, M. (2012a). *Kabbalah and Psychoanalysis*. London: Karnac.
Eigen, M. (2012b). Distinction–union structure. *Psychoanalytic Inquiry, 32*: 246–256.
Eigen, M. (2014a). *A Felt Sense: More Explorations of Psychoanalysis and Kabbalah*. London: Karnac.

Eigen, M. (2014b). *The Birth of Experience*. London: Karnac.
Eigen, M., & Govrin, A. (2007). *Conversations with Michael Eigen*. London: Karnac.
Elkin, H. (1958–1959). On the origin of the self. *Psychoanalytic Review*, 45: 57–76.
Elkin, H. (1972). On selfhood and the development of ego structures in infancy. *Psychoanalytic Review*, 59: 389–416.
Guntrip, H. (1975). My experience of analysis with Fairbairn and Winnicott—(How complete a result does psycho-analytic therapy achieve?). *International Review of Psychoanalysis*, 2: 145–156.
Intratur, J., Hare, R., Stritzke, P., Brichtswein, K., Dorfman, D., Harpur, T., Bernstein, D., Handelsman, L., Schaefer, C., Keilp, J. Rosen, J., & Machac, D. (1977). A brain imaging (single photon emission computerized tomography) study of semantic and affective processing in psychopaths. *Biological Psychiatry*, 42: 96–103.
Kuchuck, S. (Ed.) (2014). *Clinical Implications of the Psychoanalyst's Life Experience: When the Personal Becomes Professional*. New York and London: Routledge.
Lautréamont, Comte de (2004). *Maldoror and the Complete Works of the Comte de Lautréamont*, A. Lykiard (Trans.). Cambridge, MA: Exact Change.
Levinas, E. (1969). *Totality and Infinity*, A. Lignis (Trans.). Pittsburgh, PA: Duquesne University Press.
Levinas, E. (1999). *Alterity and Transcendence*. New York: Columbia University Press.
Liebes, Y. (1993). *Studies in the Zohar*. Albany, NY: State University of New York Press.
Mathers, S. L. M. (1887). *The Kabbalah Unveiled*. Whitefish, Montana: Kessinger Legacy Reprints, 2010.
Matt, D. C. (2009). *Zohar: Annotated and Explained*. Woodstock, VT: Skylight Paths.
Matte-Blanco, I. (1988). *Thinking, Feeling and Being*. London: Routledge.
Meffert, H., Gazzola, V., den Boer, J. A., Bartels, A. A. J., & Keysers, C. (2013). Reduced spontaneous but relatively normal deliberate vicarious representations in psychopathy. *Brain*, 136(8): 2550–2562.
Meltzer, D. (1994). *Sincerity and Other Works: The Collected Papers of Donald Meltzer*, A. Hahn (Ed.). London: Karnac.
Nelson, M. C., & Eigen, M. (Eds.) (1984). *Evil: Self and Culture*. New York: Human Sciences Press.
Niemera, J. C. (2011). Interview with Michael Eigen. *Psychoanalytic Perspectives*, 8(2): 259–270.

Read, H. (1965). *Icon and Idea: The Function of Art in the Development of Human Consciousness.* New York: Shocken Books.
Reik, T. (1936). *Surprise and the Psychoanalyst.* London: Kegan Paul, Trench & Trubner.
Schneerson, M. (1998). *On The Essence of Chassidus*, Y. Greenberg & S. S. Handelman, (Trans.). Brooklyn, NY: Kehot Publications Society.
Weininger, O. (1996). *Being and Not Being: Clinical Applications of the Death Instinct.* London: Taylor and Francis.
Werner, H. (1948). *Comparative Psychology of Mental Development.* Madison, CT: International Universities Press.
Williams, M. H. (2010). *Bion's Dream: A Reading of the Autobiographies.* London: Karnac.
Williams, M. H. (2013). On psychoanalytic faith. Online: http://www.artlit.info/Talks.html
Winborn, M. (Ed.) (2014). *Shared Realities: Participation Mystique and Beyond.* Carmel, CA: Fisher King Press.
Winnicott, D. W. (1953). Transitional objects and transitional phenomena: a study of the first not-me possession. *International Journal of Psychoanalysis, 34*: 89–97.
Winnicott, D. W. (1969). The use of an object and relating through identifications. *International Journal of Psychoanalysis, 50*: 711–716.
Winnicott, D. W. (1988). *Human Nature.* New York: Shocken Books.
Winnicott, D. W. (1990). *Home is Where We Start From.* London: Penguin Books.
Winnicott, D. W. (1992). *Psychoanalytic Explorations*, C. Winnicott, R. Shepherd, & M. Davis (Eds). Cambridge, MA: Harvard University Press.

INDEX

affect(ive), 30, 54, 68–69, 95, 100, 119
    attitude, 8, 94
    background, 111
    exploration, 8
    intense, 72
    keys, 77
    narratives, 1
    quality, 95
    resonance, 21
    transmission, 100
aggression, 15, 24, 39
Alcoholics Anonymous (AA), 80–81
Allen, W., 12
aloneness, 23, 29–31, 33–34, 36, 81, 116–117
anxiety, 2, 32–33, 72, 108
    psychotic, 46–47, 103

Balint, M., 80, 119
Barfield, O., 80
Bartels, A. A. J., 46
Bernstein, D., 46
Bion, W. R. (*passim*)
    cited works, xiv, 2, 19–20, 28, 31, 37–38, 40, 43–44, 52, 54, 56, 58, 60–63, 74–76, 84
    F, xii, xix, 56–57, 66
    K, 56
    –K, 56
    O, 38, 40, 57, 60–61, 66, 84
    T, 47, 57
Bohm, D., 80
Brichtswein, K., 46
Buddha, 45, 60, 93, 115

Campbell, J., 18
case studies
    Student 1, 64–66
    Student 2, 66
    Student 3, 66–67

Student 4, 67–68
Student 5, 69
Student 6, 69–70
Student 7, 70–71
Student 8, 71–72
Student 9, 72
Student 10, 72–73
Student 11, 73
Student 12, 73–74
Student 13, 74
Student 14, 74–75
catastrophe, xv, 33, 57, 64, 67, 70, 72, 101, 123–124
Chassidus, 63, 82–83
Chaya, 83
Chochma, 84
Cohen, L., 27, 70
conscious(ness), 13, 17, 68, 78, 94
   see also: unconscious(ness)
   normal, 94
   pre-, 69
   sub-, 94
   super, 94

Daat, 83
Dalai Lama, 104–105
den Boer, J. A., 46
depression, 47, 72, 84, 108, 114
   manic, 13
   position, 24, 70
development(al), 20, 24–26, 39, 78, 111
   emotional, 25, 30
   spiritual, 95
   theories, 114
   tracks, 112
Dorfman, D., 46
dream(ing), xv, 1–2, 6, 15, 17, 34, 53, 56, 73, 75, 110, 121
   experience, 17
   figure, 17
   -less sleep, xiii, 1–2, 121
   process, 56

voice, 11
work, 56, 75
Durrell, L., 11

Eddington, A. S., 61
ego, 9–10, 37, 48, 50, 111
   deformed, 50
   devil, 51
   disintegration of, 48
   empirical, 83
   psychological, 83
   psychotic, 48
   shattered, 48
   transcendental, 83
Eigen, M., xix, 1–3, 12, 14, 18, 20, 23, 25–26, 28, 32, 34–35, 38–39, 42–45, 47–48, 50, 52, 55–57, 64, 69–71, 75, 77, 79, 88–89, 91–102, 104, 107–108, 110, 113, 115, 117, 119
Elkin, H., 45, 80
Eros, 24, 87

faith, xi–xv, xvii–xix, 6, 19–20, 33, 49, 57–58, 61, 64–65, 67, 69–70, 74, 76, 78, 82–83, 101, 115, 118, 120, 124
   anti-, xi
   complex, 61
   critical, xii, 61
   cynical, xi
   dimension, 83
   naïve, xii
   natural, xi
   psychoanalytic, xii, 70
   religious, xi
   sophisticated, xii
   therapeutic, 6
First World Humanities Forum, xiii
Freud, S., xii, 10, 18, 20, 24–25, 29, 32, 34, 38–43, 47–48, 50, 53–54, 61, 82, 94, 97, 110–111, 113–115, 118, 132

frustration, 15, 24–25, 27–28, 50, 58, 63, 66, 68, 72, 75, 91

Gazzola, V., 46
Govrin, A., 14, 23
guilt, 25, 28, 44, 97, 103
Guntrip, H., 14, 39

Handelsman, L., 46
Hare, R., 46
Harpur, T., 46
hate, 10, 24, 37, 42, 50, 75, 77, 124
  see also: self
  ecstasies, 77
  frenzies, 77
  frustration-, 25
  megalomaniac, 42
  unions, 77

Intratur, J., 46
intuition, xiii, 57, 63, 73, 83
  psychoanalytic, xiii, 121

Jung, C. G., 13, 18, 83, 113–114

Kabbalah, 17–18, 38, 55, 57, 60, 63–64, 82–84, 86–87, 101, 117, 124
  Tree of Life, xv, 87
Keats, J., xii, 60
Keilp, J., 46
Kellner, Rabbi, xv, 99
Keter, 83
Keysers, C., 46
Kuchuck, S., xiii

Laing, R. D., 12–13
Lautréamont, Comte de, 43–44
Levinas, E., 3, 44
Liebes, Y., 88

Machac, D., 46
Malchut, 82, 88
Mathers, S. L. M., 88

Matt, D. C., 88
Matte-Blanco, I., 80
Meffert, H., 46
Meltzer, D., 37, 73
Milner, M., 17, 32, 38, 101

Nefesh, 82
Nelson, M. C., 42
Neshama, 82
New Hope Guild, 107–108, 114
New York University Contemplative Studies Project, 18, 117
Niemera, J. C., xvi

object, 23–25, 28, 30, 33, 62, 74, 115
  aloneness, 33
  contact, 26
  discussion, 28
  formulation, 24, 28
  loved, 75
  of destruction, 25
  subject–, 5
  transitional, 14
  use of, xiv
  world, 25
Odenheimer, M., xv, 91

paranoid, 94, 103, 108
  aspect, 77
  schizoid, 24, 70, 114
psyche, 5, 8, 16, 20, 23, 33–35, 45, 56, 59, 64–65, 67, 71, 75, 78, 79, 97, 108–110, 116–118, 123
psychosis, xv, 20, 24–25, 32, 37, 45, 47–48, 79, 119

Quran, 103

Read, H., 78
reality, xiv–xv, 10, 13–15, 21–22, 24–29, 35, 38, 41, 56, 59, 61–63, 76, 84, 91
  emotional, 6, 17, 19, 38, 56–57, 62, 67, 123

fundamental, 31, 60, 84
infinite, 84
living, 35
measureless, 62
open, 6
outer, xix, 30
  inner–, 81
principle, 24
psychic, xiii, 8, 14, 20, 35, 56, 58, 115
spiritual, 98
ultimate, 38
Reik, T., 16
Rickman, J., 16
Rosen, J., 46
Ruach, 82

Schaefer, C., 46
Schneerson, M., xv, 63, 99, 104–105
self, xii, xvii, 8–9, 15–17, 24, 42, 48, 50, 75, 77, 81, 85, 99, 112, 119, 121
  -awareness, 80
  -centred, 10
  -crippling, 10
  dark, 69
  -destruction, 5, 105
  -feeling, 31, 110
  -giving, 4
  -hating, 100, 105
  idiosyncratic, 21
  -images, 100
  -interest, 4, 44, 47
  -intoxication, 103
  loss of, 79
  -orientated, xvi
  -persecution, 84
  -righteousness, 103
  -selective, 59
Sephirot, 83, 89
Shakespeare, W., 41–42, 53–54, 97, 103
Shechinah, xv, 88–89
Stritzke, P., 46

The Bible, 7, 59, 103
Tiferet, 87
trauma(tic), 33, 52, 61–62, 72, 95, 111, 123
  components, 52
  deep, 39, 100–102
  explosiveness, 52
  hits, xiii
  post-, 52
  primal, 43, 61, 123
  severe, 24
Trungpa, C., xv, 13, 104

unconscious(ness), 2, 13, 20, 28, 30, 41, 69, 78, 93, 100, 104
  see also: conscious(ness)

Weininger, O., 36
Werner, H., 80
Williams, M. H., xiv
Winborn, M., xv
Winnicott, C., xiii–xiv, 28–29
Winnicott, D. W. (*passim*)
  cited works, 14, 24, 26, 28, 30–33, 39, 46, 78
Wittgenstein, L., 53, 74

yechida, 82–84

Zohar, xv, 17–18, 60, 88–89, 101–102, 117